TEACH LIKE
SOCRATES

FOR GRADES 7–12

TEACH LIKE SOCRATES

Guiding Socratic Dialogues & Discussions in the Classroom

ERICK WILBERDING, PH.D.

PRUFROCK PRESS INC.
WACO, TEXAS

To Iosi, Samuel, and Linda

Library of Congress Cataloging-in-Publication Data

Wilberding, Erick.
Teach like Socrates : guiding Socratic dialogues and discussions in the classroom / by Erick Wilberding, Ph.D.
  pages cm
ISBN 978-1-61821-143-9 (pbk.)
1. Questioning. 2. Interaction analysis in education. 3. Socrates. I. Title.
LB1027.44.W47 2014
371.3'7--dc23
                      2013035551

Front cover:
David, Jacques Louis (1748-1825). The Death of Socrates. 1787. Oil on canvas, 51 x 77 1/4 in. (129.5 x 196.2 em).
Catharine Lorillard Wolfe Collection, Wolfe Fund, 1931 (31.45).
The Metropolitan Museum of Art, New York, NY, U.S.A.
Image copyright © The Metropolitan Museum of Art. Image source: Art Resource, NY

Edited by Bethany Johnsen

Layout and cover design by Raquel Trevino

ISBN-13: 978-1-61821-143-9

At the time of this book's publication, all facts and figures cited are the most current available; all telephone numbers, addresses, and website URLs are accurate and active; all publications, organizations, websites, and other resources exist as described in this book; and all have been verified. The author and Prufrock Press make no warranty or guarantee concerning the information and materials given out by organizations or content found at websites, and we are not responsible for any changes that occur after this book's publication. If you find an error or believe that a resource listed here is not as described, please contact Prufrock Press.

Prufrock Press Inc.
P.O. Box 8813
Waco, TX 76714-8813
Phone: (800) 998-2208
Fax: (800) 240-0333
http://www.prufrock.com

TABLE OF CONTENTS

Introduction The Fourth "R"—Reasoning 1

Chapter 1 "I am a kind of gadfly":
The Life of Socrates 13

Chapter 2 How to Examine Life:
The Two Socratic Methods 21

Chapter 3 Be Careful What You Ask For:
Preparing a Socratic Dialogue 39

Chapter 4 Take the Students With You:
Conducting a Socratic Dialogue 59

Chapter 5 Cultivating Gadflies:
Teaching Students the Socratic Method 69

Chapter 6 Searching and Testing:
Preparing a Socratic Discussion 89

Chapter 7 Splitting the Education Atom:
Conducting a Socratic Discussion 99

Chapter 8 Conclusion:
Thinking and Arguing Together 115

References 123

Appendix A Further Reading 131

Appendix B Planning Templates 133

Appendix C Suggestions for Discussion Texts 143

About the Author 147

Common Core State Standards Alignment 149

THE FOURTH "R"— REASONING

The 21st-century world is flooded with information. We can know almost anything instantly. But what is important to know? How do we know that it is important? How do we analyze and evaluate it? How do we apply it in new and unforeseen situations? How do we collaborate in analyzing, evaluating, and applying our knowledge? How can we create new knowledge?

Each subject in school, shaped by its assumptions, definitions, and principles, answers these questions through different methods. In science classes, students create knowledge through application of the scientific method; in literature classes, through imagination and analysis of language; in mathematics classes, through meticulous reasoning with numbers, figures, and formulas; in history classes, through the careful sifting of primary and secondary sources to separate opinion from fact, understand cause and effect, and so assemble a plausible view of the past. And, upon more careful examination, there is usually a unique blending of qualitative and quantitative methods in each field. We see that imagination is important for the progress of science, even as meticulous reasoning is crucial for the analysis of poetry. There is usually the conviction that knowledge is open to revision by new facts or understandings. Knowledge is dynamic and growing.

In each subject, critical thinking is a core skill. This skill empowers students to navigate the widening ocean of information and data and to arrive at new destinations. Tony Wagner (2008), the first Innovation Education Fellow at the Technology and Entrepreneurship Center at Harvard, has identified critical thinking and problem solving as the very first survival skill for the 21st-century. Technology progresses at an exponential rate, and our world is changing more rapidly than in the past. I believe that Socrates would have agreed with Professor Wagner. Certainly the Socratic Method focuses on this immensely important skill.

In 5th century Athens, Socrates practiced a method of teaching critical thinking that remains the basis of much meaningful education today. Socratic pedagogy focuses on questioning, and especially on facilitating higher level thinking by skillful inductive questioning. Inductive questioning moves from premise to premise to a discovery. If done at the proper pace and in the proper tone, this manner of teaching stimulates and guides students to think more critically. They learn how to examine assumptions, principles, reasoning, and evidence; how to consider implications and consequences; and how to imagine and critique alternatives. Done correctly, the Socratic Method empowers students to think and problem-solve.

The best guides to the Socratic Method are the dialogues of Plato. Studied largely in philosophy departments, these dialogues today are the most neglected classics of pedagogy. Reading them as a teacher, one can only be fascinated by the pedagogical craft of Socrates, his incisive analysis and evaluation within a shared investigation. The primary purpose of this book is to show teachers how to question inductively in this Socratic manner.

Socrates is the most famous teacher of antiquity, but, surprisingly enough, his method is not well known in practical detail. Many associate it with legal education, and perhaps have even caught glimpses of it in old movies or television series like *The Paper Chase*. Others believe, incorrectly, that it is simply synonymous with questioning, and is best used for drilling and quizzing for information, an exercise for recalling facts. In reality, the Socratic Method has been adapted for different contexts, from elementary education to legal and business training in graduate school, and it consistently guides students into higher level thinking.

Socratic Method in Recent History

One catches flashes of the Socratic Method in history. In his youth, Benjamin Franklin read Xenophon and playfully practiced the Socratic Method (Houston, 2004). Isaac Watts praised it in *The Improvement of the Mind* (1741), declaring, among other things, that

> it leads the learner into the knowledge of truth as it were by his own invention, which is a very pleasing thing to human nature; and by questions pertinently and artificially pro-

posed, it does as effectually draw him on to discover his own mistakes, which he is more easily persuaded to relinquish when he seems to have discovered them himself (p. 171).

In the late 19th and early 20th centuries, when great strides were made in Plato scholarship, we see the Socratic Method always distinguished from catechetical questioning and extolled by different religious educators, such as Sir John Adams (n.d.), whose small volume contains three example dialogues. The Socratic Method is mentioned and fulsomely praised, but not extensively developed, in the popular manuals on recitation intended for secondary school teachers. Charles A. McMurry and Frank M. McMurry (1903), for instance, treat it briefly and with admiration in *The Method of the Recitation*. George Herbert Betts (1910) also presents the Socratic Method, characterizing it as "the very height of good teaching" (pp. 30–33). Herman Harrell Horne (1916), who was professor of the history of education and the history of philosophy at New York University, presented the Socratic Method briefly in a slender book. Samuel Hamilton (1906) explained very well some of the salient characteristics and benefits of the method. Most authors remark that it is difficult to learn. Samuel Chester Parker (1920) is quite negative about the Socratic Method, but, judging from the two simplistic and caustic observations he makes, I believe that he fails to understand thoroughly its utility. We should keep in mind too that recitation and the Socratic Method are not synonyms. Recitation was a common activity in secondary schools, and the Socratic Method could fit within this activity, if the teacher mastered it.

Much better known is the law school adaption of the Socratic Method. In 1870, Christopher Columbus Langdell pioneered the case method of studying law at Harvard University (Kimball, 2009). He believed that law was a science and appellate cases were the best materials for learning this science. In the classroom, the task was to isolate the most significant facts of a case and then to detect the reasoning for the judge's ruling. Langdell guided analysis through inductive questioning. At first controversial, the case method gradually gained popularity, and by the time of Langdell's death in 1906, it was regarded as the very best method for learning the law. The boast was that it made you think like a lawyer.

The experience of the Socratic Method in the legal classroom depended much on the expertise and temperament of the questioning professor. Some professors, regrettably for the students and for the reputation of the Socratic Method, could be ruthless. In the late 1960s, protest against the Socratic Method gained momentum, although its defenders (e.g., Areeda, whose 1996 outline makes very good reading) could be found at all points of the spectrum, from liberal to conservative. But its use has decreased in law schools (Kerr, 1999). In general, where it survives today, it is used in a softer manner and in conjunction with other teaching strategies.

Socratic questioning is also used at Harvard Business School. Based on the examination and evaluation of cases, it fosters more open exchanges between students and between the students and the professor. Several excellent books have been published about this, such as *Education for Judgment* (Christensen, Garvin, & Sweet, 1991). Not as rigid as legal Socratic questioning, it probes analysis, evaluation, and decision-making in response to real-life business cases. "What would you do in this situation?" is the basic question, and this is followed up with questions for clarification, justification, connections, and extension.

One also sees this approach, choreographing soft collisions of opinions and ideas, in Harvard professor Michael Sandel's admirable and well-known undergraduate classes, videos of which are available online (see http://www.justiceharvard.org).

There are other excellent adaptations of the Socratic Method. The Hungarian mathematician George Pólya (1957) further elaborated the method into a broader heuristic in *How to Solve It*, first published in 1945. Pólya outlined a four-step method, each step having several facets, for solving not only mathematical problems, but any problem. The first step is to understand the problem, the next is to understand the relation of the data to the unknown and to devise a plan (analyze), then to carry out the plan (synthesize), and finally to examine the solution. In an earlier publication, he summarized the process as "Understand, Take Apart, Put Together, Check" (Pólya & Anning, 1935, p. 273). In this process, the teacher guides the student through questions to make his own discoveries. The epigraph of another work expresses Pólya's inductive Socratic approach: "What is good education? Giving systematically opportunity to the student to discover things by himself" (Pólya & Szegö, 1972/1998, p. vi).

A broader Socratic approach developed in the Great Books discussion groups that began at Columbia University after World War I. In the wake of changes to the university curriculum, there was concern that many monuments of Western culture were being neglected. Novelist and professor John Erskine began the Great Books discussion groups, which became extraordinarily popular, and this work was continued and considerably expanded in the next decades, especially through the efforts of Mortimer Adler and Robert Maynard Hutchins (Beam, 2008). These discussions were critical conversations on the work developed in reference to a handful of thematic questions, prodded into further analysis by two leaders. To facilitate the expansion of the program, Adler (1946) wrote a manual for leaders.

We have reviewed very briefly how the Socratic Method has been used in the past, as well as in higher education and adult education. But can it also be used in elementary or secondary education? Certainly, it can. The Socratic Method is one of many forms of inductive teaching or discovery learning that allow students to make a discovery through their own efforts, not through the passive reception of information.

Advocated by Jerome Bruner and many other psychologists and educationists, discovery learning has made great strides since the 1960s, finding expression in social studies, math, language, and science curricula. A variety of teaching models have developed inductive strategies for the classroom for individual and group learning (Joyce & Calhoun, 1998).

It is odd that the Socratic Method, which at its best provides a paradigm for such exploration, has not been widely understood and adapted for daily use. One outstanding exception is seen in the influential work of Hilda Taba (1902–1967). Originally from Estonia, Taba completed a doctorate in educational philosophy at Columbia University and soon afterwards became involved in a research study on curriculum (Krull, 2003). Curriculum development remained a focus through the next decades, leading her to develop her ideas regarding the teaching of thinking. Her method of inductive questioning to develop concepts, generalizations, and applications is patient, wise, as well as strikingly and unmistakably Socratic. Through inductive questions, the teacher gently guides elementary school students to develop concepts and generalizations, and then to apply these in a consistent manner (Durkin, 1993; Taba, 1967).

Linda Elder and Richard Paul have made a strong and excellent contribution to fostering Socratic education through many books and articles as well as through the Critical Thinking Foundation, which energetically propagates their Socratic ideals and practices throughout the curriculum (see http://www.criticalthinking.org). In particular, they elucidate several basic principles of Socratic questioning in a short series of exemplary articles (Elder & Paul, 1998; Paul & Elder, 2007a, 2007b, 2008). Other books and articles encourage the transfer of critical thinking skills to daily life. Elder and Paul's efforts to transform education from teacher information-sharing to autonomous construction of knowledge by the student are well-known (Moseley et al., 2005).

Another notable contribution was made by Mortimer Adler, who adapted his classically oriented educational ideas to secondary education with the founding of the Paideia Program in the 1980s (Adler, 1982, 1983, 1984a). Socratic coaching and discussion, along the same principles and procedures of the Great Books discussion program, are central teaching activities. Advanced today by the Paideia Center under the guidance of Terry Roberts and Laura Billings, who have also authored texts furthering Adler's ideas and discussion principles, this program continues to impact education.

Socratic Seminars remain an excellent method for organizing discussions in high school (Ball & Brewer, 2000; Copeland, 2005). But at the same time, they somehow do not seem exactly Socratic when compared with the dialogues of Plato and Xenophon. Mortimer Adler and Charles van Doren (1984) in fact wrote that

> Plato's dialogues, in so many of which Socrates appears as the interlocutor, do not portray him as a seminar leader. Nor do they describe the kind of seminar discussions that should play so central a part in a Paideia school.
>
> In questioning those with whom he talked, Socrates sought for answers that would clarify ideas—the idea of justice, of love, of piety or virtue. He did not assign books to be read for a seminar session in which he would ask questions in order to achieve an understanding of what had been read, nor did he raise issues for the participants to argue about (p. 15).

The Socratic Seminar, or Socratic Circle, uses the adjective "Socratic" as a broad synonym for "organized with questions," but this does not mean, I think, that the questions are similar in form or sequence to those Socrates once asked. In the contemporary format used in secondary schools, Socratic Seminar questions generally are topical or thematic. The aim is to have an open and critical conversation that delves meaningfully into the text. The fishbowl technique, which has one circle of conversing students surrounded by another circle of observing students, was an innovation of Training Groups (T Groups) borrowed by the Socratic Seminar. In one variation, unlike the Great Books discussion groups, which had two active leaders, the teacher does not intervene in the discussion at all.

In education, one can see the footprints of Socrates wherever there is systematic questioning. In classrooms, this questioning can be directed at an individual in a dialogue, or at a class in discussion. In a broader perspective, these can be the Essential Questions that guide the backward curriculum design advocated by Wiggins and McTighe (2011). Or, in a more narrow perspective, this systematic questioning can direct students in the same way that a personal trainer or coach assists an athlete or group of athletes.

This book is intended for learning this method of systematic inductive questioning, whose purpose, as has always been recognized, is not imparting information but teaching others to think critically about it. Socratic dialogue continues to merit a role in education, but it is difficult to learn and requires practice. In the past, it held a small place in treatments of traditional recitation, but recitation itself has largely dropped out of use in the United States, and Socratic questioning in the more strict sense has also. But everyone recognizes that questioning is perennially relevant, and the Socratic Method, in its strict sense, is essentially the art of the question.

The Socratic Method:
Higher Level Thinking

One can frame the Socratic Method very well with Bloom's revised taxonomy. In 1956, Benjamin S. Bloom's edition of *Taxonomy of Educational Objectives* appeared and in succeeding decades became an extraordinarily helpful resource for classifying the goals of tests and curriculum design in general, both at the university and in primary and secondary education. In 2001, Anderson et al. revised the taxonomy in light of more recent research about teaching and learning. Instead of a continuum from Knowledge to Evaluation, the revised taxonomy articulated teaching objectives according to the cognitive process engaged and the type of knowledge concerned. It allows one to clearly align teaching objectives, activities, and assessment, so that there is a conscious understanding that the learner is challenged and evaluated in a consistent manner.

The Cognitive Process Dimension arranges the thought processes across a hierarchy. Formerly these categories were ordered Knowledge, Comprehension, Application, Analysis, Synthesis, and Evaluation. In the new taxonomy, the order as well as the nomenclature has changed to Remember, Understand, Apply, Analyze, Evaluate, and Create. The revision is more consciously constructive and focused upon retention and transferable learning.

The Knowledge Dimension has four categories: Factual Knowledge, Conceptual Knowledge, Procedural Knowledge, and Metacognitive Knowledge.

The entire new taxonomy joins the Cognitive Process and Knowledge Dimensions in order to express teaching objectives. In expressing a teaching objective, one typically uses a verb and a noun or noun phrase. The verb expresses the cognitive process, and the noun or noun phrase expresses the knowledge dimension. For example, *Students will learn to recognize the*

Spectrum of knowledge
Factual – conceptual – procedural – metacognitive

characteristics of Renaissance art. The verb *recognize* expresses the cognitive process, which is related to the Remembering category. The phrase *the characteristics of Renaissance art* is related to Conceptual Knowledge because it expresses a classification.

As mentioned before, through the taxonomy one can better understand learning objectives, activities, and assessment. Among the activities or assessments, one can also classify the objectives of classroom questions. For example, questions eliciting facts test memory alone and, while this does have a certain utility and can demonstrate retention, it is not distinctively Socratic. Moving forward along the continuum of the taxonomy, one passes into questions that elicit deeper understanding and more accurate application, as well as more meticulous analysis and evaluation. They also can help in creating new knowledge. In the end, however, single questions (even the important questions of *how* and *why*) asked in isolation are not exactly Socratic.

But more extended sequences of inductive questions can become Socratic. As sequences of inductive questions move along the cognitive continuum and guide the learner to higher level thinking, they become increasingly Socratic in the stricter sense. As the sequences move beyond the factual dimension, passing into conceptual, procedural, and metacognitive knowledge, fostering in the end heightened self-awareness and self-knowledge as a learner, they become increasingly Socratic.

In this book I distinguish two Socratic methods, both of which can be understood through Bloom's taxonomy. The first focuses on the articulation, application, and analysis of concepts, and the second on careful guidance through a method or process. Each is oriented to higher level thinking. Each can lead to creative thinking before new problems and situations. In other words, the Socratic Method can validly appeal to any section of Bloom's taxonomy.

Daniel Kahneman (2011) and other proponents of dual process theory discern two interacting systems of thinking (Myers, 2004). The first system is rapid, emotional, intuitive, nonverbal, self-evident (requiring no justification), and given to generalizing. The second system is slow and at times lazy, logical, justified with evidence, and differentiated; that is, it makes distinctions and does not overgeneralize. The Socratic Method guides careful thinking in the second system without being overly distracted by the first.

How This Book Is Organized

In Chapter 1, I review the life of Socrates, who walked through Athens and, in the most unpretentious manner, engaged people of all types in dialogues to sift out the truth of claims of knowledge. In a sense, without being lazy, he was the system 2 thinking for the city of Athens. He made distinctions and applied logic to arrive at appropriate conclusions, which did not usually please his interlocutors. Accused of corrupting the youth and not believing in the gods, he was tried, found guilty, and condemned to death.

In Chapter 2, I distinguish two Socratic methods. Using examples from the dialogues of Plato and Xenophon, particularly excerpts from *Alcibiades* and *Meno*, I show that the first method has six basic characteristics and inductively examines claims and concepts that are specially meaningful to the other person. Examining a well-known passage from *Meno*, I show that the second method, which is later further articulated by the mathematician Pólya, inductively guides the student through a process to obtain a solution to a problem or the examination of an issue. The application of the elements and principles of the two methods can mix and vary according to the individual and the objectives of the dialogue.

In Chapters 3 and 4, I explain how to prepare and conduct a Socratic dialogue in the classroom. In the well-known teaching formula, *I do, We do, You do*, Socratic instruction builds the bridge from *We do* to *You do*. For Socratic Method 1, you begin by assembling a Dialogue Binder of materials. There are three steps in preparation. With Bloom's revised taxonomy, you select precise objectives. Form follows function in a Socratic dialogue; its versatile elements can be combined and applied in many different ways, depending on the objectives. Backward planning is necessary, and you must envision the final destination as well as the major stops along the way. After brainstorming, research, and reflection, you construct an inductive outline that guides to these stops and opens to analysis. Socratic Method 2 is easier to prepare, for you know the process to be taught and the only challenge is to phrase and rephrase questions to give just enough help without giving too much. In delivering the lesson, you must create a psychologically safe environment. Always listen attentively to the responses of the students. And, although you have planned carefully, you should expect to explore other paths. You should clarify, challenge, connect, and explore consequences. It is helpful along the way to introduce some of the basic terms of argument construction. Chapter 4 ends with the 10 Commandments of Socratic Questioning.

In Chapter 5, I explain how to teach students to plan and conduct a short dialogue with Socratic Method 1. Students learn what they do. Empowering the students to ask the inductive questions allows them to become more equal collaborators in Socratic exploration, not dependent upon the teacher. I explain how to teach the students about induction and, using passages from dialogues by Xenophon and Plato, review the characteristics of Socratic Method 1. I review some of the mistakes that can surface in sequences of questions. We look at fallacies such as the slippery slope as well as order bias. Students understand the Socratic Method better when they ask the questions.

In Chapters 6 and 7, I explain how to prepare and conduct a Socratic discussion as well as how to further develop discussion skills. After the intensity of Socratic dialogue, one approaches more open discussion with a heightened awareness of the possibilities of questions. In preparation for discussion, one formulates content, exploratory, and analytic questions. Discussion games reinforce fundamental skills necessary for genuine collaborative work. Students can increasingly attain the confidence, freedom, and expertise to conduct their own discussions without any teacher intervention.

Appendix A: Further Reading discusses the best texts for teachers to consult to learn more about the Socratic Method. Appendix B provides templates for your use in planning Socratic dialogue and Appendix C lists suitable texts for class discussions.

Toward the Socratic Classroom

My own quest for learning the Socratic Method led me to the original sources, namely the works of Plato and Xenophon. In reading these works, having spent many years in the classroom, I was often struck by the teaching style of Socrates. Making allowances for the literary and dramatic qualities of the dialogues—and admitting that, in some dialogues, the use of the leading question becomes monotonous and would be ineffective in the classroom—I nonetheless often caught glimpses of an ancient teacher of great originality and charm at work. Socrates engaged the individual and led him to greater understanding. I saw differentiated instruction that accepts where the student is and then leads him forward. I feel this extraordinary method is not adequately represented in current pedagogical literature. It is a unique way of teaching that can have a positive and lasting impact on learners and teachers alike, whether this education takes place in the home (i.e., homeschooling) or in the community. Meeting Socrates changes your way of thinking for the better.

In writing about Socrates, I almost feel as if I am trespassing in the Promised Land of philosophy. But this book is not written for philosophers or historians of philosophy, some of whom debate different understandings of the Socratic Method and throw light on different aspects of it. I do make use of the dialogue *Alcibiades*, whose authenticity is discussed, because it offers much to the teacher wishing to learn more about Socratic Method (and it is very enjoyable to read).

Nor is this a book of educational theory. It is intended as a pragmatic book to help teachers and students acquire the complex skills needed for truly Socratic inquiry.

My principal aim is to make the Socratic methods accessible to the general teacher and student. For this reason, I have shunned the use of more specialized vocabulary one encounters in the literature about the Socratic Method (e.g., *elenchus, eristic, dialectic, aporia, maieutic*, etc.). I have sought to isolate the central characteristics and dynamics of Socratic teaching and explain them in common language.

The Socratic Method is not only about the destination; it is about the inductive journey, critically encountering ideas and experiences that give delineation and meaning to any claim, concept, issue, or problem. At its best, once the students have understood its elements and assimilated its dynamic, Socratic Method is not guided inquiry, but shared inquiry.

More than 40 years ago, Postman and Weingartner (1969) exclaimed that "the most important ability man has yet developed—the art and science of asking questions—is not taught in school!" (p. 23). My hope is that this volume contributes to teaching that complex art and science.

Chapter 1

"I AM A KIND OF GADFLY"
The Life of Socrates

> He often said, that he wondered at those who made stone statues, when he saw how careful they were that the stone should be like the man it was intended to represent, but how careless they were of themselves, as to guarding against being like the stone.
>
> —Diogenes Laertius

Highly intelligent, shrewd, playful, stubborn, physically and morally courageous, frugal, single-minded, notoriously ugly and chubby, charming, funny, and lovable, one of the great philosophers and teachers of the ancient world, Socrates lived in Athens during the 5th century BCE, a very special time. By far Athens did not have a perfect democracy, for there was slavery and women had no rights. But long strides were made in many spheres, and Socrates witnessed them. Like the general and statesman Pericles, the playwrights Sophocles and Euripides, the architects Ictinus and Callicrates, the sculptor Phidias, the painters Zeuxis and Polygnotus, and the historian Thucydides, Socrates contributed to the Athenian Golden Age. His contribution was unique, turning philosophy in a new direction with a new method of inquiry. His method has inspired and guided teachers for centuries.

How can we know anything about Socrates? There are several ancient sources. Aristophanes (c. 423 B.C.E./2005) ridiculed Socrates at length in his comic play *The Clouds* and mentioned him in other plays. Xenophon (c. 371 B.C.E./1994), a soldier and writer, knew the philosopher and wrote dialogues as well as a memoir of his life. Plato, one of the greatest philosophers of the ancient world, also knew Socrates and later made him the central figure in most of his many dialogues. Aristotle made remarks about Socrates (Guthrie, 1971, p. 35–39). There are also fragments in works by other ancient philosophers, as well as an ancient biography by Diogenes Laertius (c. 225/1915).

There are issues in interpreting these ancient sources, for the different portraits do not neatly align. How much truth is there in the comic play by Aristophanes? Is the Socrates of Xenophon too simplistic? Is the Socrates of Plato only a mouthpiece for Plato's own theories? Are the later fragments cluttered with legends? Scholars have sifted through the enigmatic details and have made many excellent distinctions. In general, many regard the figure of Socrates by Plato in his earlier dialogues as being closest to the historical person. From all of the sources, despite the lacunae, we can assemble an intriguing portrait of the greatest teacher of the ancient world. In effect, we can piece together a mosaic from the tesserae of several other mosaics.

The Stone Worker's Son

Socrates was born in 469 B.C.E., the son of Sophroniscus and Phaenarete, in Alopeke, a district of Athens. Sophroniscus was a stone worker or sculptor, and it is probable that Socrates learned this art from his father. In antiquity, many attributed a clothed group of the Three Graces on the Acropolis to Socrates. His mother was a midwife, an occupation that provided Socrates (or Plato) with a metaphor for his own role as an educator, someone who will bring to light the ideas of others.

As a young man, Socrates studied natural philosophy, speculating about the nature of the physical world, but he grew frustrated with the irresolvable contradictions between the different schools of thought. It seemed that no natural philosopher could attain certainty. In the *Phaedo*, he confesses that "finally I became convinced that I have no natural aptitude at all for that kind of investigation" (Plato, c. 383 B.C.E./1997; 96c). So he turned his mind to other problems.

Later Cicero famously said that Socrates brought philosophy down from the skies. He turned philosophical inquiry from natural phenomena to the problems of the moral life. The questions now became: What is a good life? What is virtue? Can one learn virtue? Socrates became the first moral philosopher.

But he did not escape into solitude to scribble his philosophical thoughts. On the contrary, whenever and wherever he encountered anyone who made a claim to knowledge, he began a shared examination of the claim. "Let's consider the question together," he would say. Social status, place, and time did not matter. In the agora, in the streets, in homes and shops and the wrestling school, in the morning, afternoon, or evening, Socrates examined and evaluated claims and issues with people. Not at all a remote professor in an ivory tower, he moved among the people. He was gregarious.

Unlike the Sophists, Socrates had no school and did not even regard himself as a teacher. He did not lecture, and in fact distrusted speeches or lectures, for they sailed too far and fast on rhetoric and evaded the closer scrutiny of their cargo of ideas. He conversed with the other person and was genuinely interested in what that person thought and felt. He professed no doctrine and accepted no fees for his discussions. With all of his formidable intellectual gifts and comic appearance, he also was irreverent and ironic. He poked fun at others.

Perhaps this irreverence and gregariousness explains why young men flocked to listen to his examinations and to learn his method of questioning. Plato was one of them, and so was Xenophon. In the dialogues of Plato, one can see Socrates coaching young men to ask questions of those who made claims. Young men learned how to question adeptly. The Socratic Method was the instrument used to weigh evidence, to examine reasoning, and to discover the grains of truth.

After Socrates had achieved a measure of fame or notoriety in Athens, the comic poet Aristophanes satirized him in his play *The Clouds*, first performed in 423 B.C.E., in which the character of the philosopher has a school and worships the clouds. In the very first scene in which Socrates appears, he is suspended absurdly in a basket above the stage, intent on worshipping the clouds. In his school, he teaches his pupils how to make the weak argument appear stronger, how to avoid payment of debts, and how to intimidate their parents into doing their will. The comedy fanned Socrates' reputation for frivolous speculation and worship and for misleading the youth. Later, Socrates said that it contributed to his condemnation.

The philosopher could remain immobile in contemplation for many hours, even through the night. He also claimed to perceive an inner voice, a divine sign that from time to time inspired him to select a course of action, something that has always provoked comments. Eccentric and extraordinary, he was a charismatic figure in Athens. He was lovable. He married Xanthippe and they had three sons, Lamprocles, Sophroniscus, and Menexenus.

During the Peloponnesian War, the long conflict between Athens and Sparta, Socrates exhibited great physical courage. He was an armed foot soldier and drew attention to himself because of his physical endurance and toughness, dressing simply and wearing no shoes even when trudging through snow. At the battle at Potidaea in 432 B.C.E., he saved the life of the young Alcibiades. In 424 B.C.E., when he was in his mid-40s, he fought at Delium, where the Athenians were defeated and forced to retreat. Two years later, he fought at Amphipolis. Alcibiades praises him in *Symposium:*

> . . . we served together and shared the same mess. Now, first, he took the hardships of the campaign much better than I ever did—much better, in fact, than anyone in the whole army. When we were cut off from our supplies, as often happens in the field, no one else stood up to hunger as well as he did. And yet he was the one man who could really enjoy a feast; and though he didn't much want to drink, when he had to, he could drink the best of us under the table. Still, and most amazingly, no one ever saw him drunk (as we'll straightaway put to the test).
>
> Add to this his amazing resistance to the cold—and, let me tell you, the winter there is something awful. Once, I remember, it was frightfully cold; no one so much as stuck his nose outside. If we absolutely had to leave our tent, we wrapped ourselves in anything we could lay our hands on and tied extra pieces of felt or sheepskin over our boots. Well, Socrates went out in that weather wearing nothing but this same old light cloak, and even in bare feet he made better progress on the ice than the other soldiers did in their boots. You should have seen the looks they gave him; they thought he was only doing it to spite them! (Plato c. 385 B.C.E./1997l, 220a–220c)

Socrates's friend Chaerephon traveled to Delphi to ask the oracle of Apollo, "Who is the wisest of men?" Cryptically, the oracle replied that none was wiser than Socrates. This answer perplexed and tormented Socrates, who was certain he knew nothing. He reasoned that his wisdom consisted in the awareness that he knew nothing, whereas many others did not have this same awareness. The oracle provided a new motivation for his activity. His keen awareness of his own ignorance compelled him to examine others. His examinations led others to take the first small step: the realization that one knows nothing.

Socrates did not record any of his ideas in writing. Other philosophers had written poetry or treatises to preserve or propagate their thought. Plato later expressed skepticism about the possibility that writing can preserve thought, so easily misunderstood in its subtleties. One needs to be able to question, to clarify, to challenge, to connect, to unravel the possible consequences. Written texts cannot answer questions as a living person can.

Although he thought and argued about ethics and politics, Socrates did not enter political life. But he fulfilled his civic duties with integrity and courage. In 406 B.C.E., when a group of generals was accused of causing the death of soldiers, he alone refused to break the Athenian law and condemn the group. Nonetheless the group, whose trial lasted a single day, was condemned and executed.

Two years later, after the defeat of Athens in the Peloponnesian War, Sparta installed the Thirty Tyrants to govern Athens. The most ruthless leader was Critias, a former pupil of Socrates and one of the uncles of Plato. Intensely undemocratic, the Thirty restricted rights to the wealthy and put to death more than 1,500 people in order to seize their money and possessions. In this climate of intrigue and violence, Socrates refused to illegally arrest the wealthy foreigner Leon of Salamis. Xenophon wrote that the Thirty forbade Socrates to teach (c. 371 B.C.E./1994). In 403 B.C.E., the Thirty were defeated, with Clitias killed in battle.

Arrest, Trial, and Death

Some scholars suggest that the hostility to Socrates intensified because his former pupil Critias was the leader of the Thirty. Another well-known former pupil, Alcibiades, defected to the Spartans, then to the Persians, and finally returned to the Athenian side before his death in 404 B.C.E. Socrates was associated with these two traitorous men in the popular mind. In reality, the Thirty were hostile to Socrates, who had refused to be complicit in the arrests of innocent people.

Socrates also alienated powerful figures through his examinations in obedience to the oracle of Delphi:

> As a result of this investigation, men of Athens, I acquired much unpopularity, of a kind that is hard to deal with and is a heavy burden; many slanders came from these people and a reputation for wisdom, for in each case the bystanders thought that I myself possessed the wisdom that I proved that my interlocutor did not have. (Plato, c. 360 B.C.E./1997a, 23a)

In the spring of 399 B.C.E., three men, Meletus, Anytus, and Lycon, brought charges against Socrates, and he was arrested. The formal charges were that he did not believe in the gods and that he corrupted the youth. Socrates could have gone into voluntary exile, but chose instead to remain in Athens for the trial.

The trial took place before 500 citizens, not a genuine representation of the city, but a group of impoverished men who needed the stipend for jury duty. The trial must have had speeches of accusation and defense, and perhaps witnesses were called. No transcript exists for what Socrates uttered, but both Plato and Xenophon composed speeches purporting to recreate the speech he gave before the court. In Plato's *Apology*, Socrates masterfully dissects the charges against him and shows their lack of substance and logic. He attacks the sincerity of Meletus on the charge of corruption of the youth. He then questions him on the charge of atheism and dismantles that accusation. He also distances himself from the vicious conduct of his former pupil Critias. And famously he claims that he is not a teacher (see Plato, c. 360 B.C.E./1997b, 33b).

He knew his examinations were necessary and beneficial to the state. He tells them he is "a kind of gadfly":

> I was attached to this city by the god—though it seems a ridic-
> ulous thing to say—as upon a great and noble horse which
> was somewhat sluggish because of its size and needed to be
> stirred up by a kind of gadfly. (Plato, c. 360 B.C.E./1997b,
> 30e)

But the jury finds him guilty nonetheless, and Meletus cruelly demands the death penalty. Before closing his defense, Socrates says:

> Perhaps someone might say: But Socrates, if you leave us will
> you not be able to live quietly, without talking? Now this is
> the most difficult point on which to convince some of you. If
> I say that it is impossible for me to keep quiet because that
> means disobeying the god, you will not believe me and will
> think I am being ironical. On the other hand, if I say that
> it is the greatest good for a man to discuss virtue every day
> and those other things about which you hear me conversing
> and testing myself and others, for the unexamined life is not
> worth living for men, you will believe me even less. (Plato, c.
> 360 B.C.E./1997b, 38a)

His phrase "The unexamined life is not worth living" expresses his uncompromising search for truth and has echoed to the present. Despite Socrates's poignant and able defense, the Athenian assembly was not convinced. They condemned the 70-year-old philosopher to death. Socrates accepted the verdict with a composure and mildness that has always provoked admiration. He looks forward to the conversations he may have in the underworld:

> Most important, I could spend my time testing and examining people there, as I do here, as to who among them is wise, and who thinks he is, but is not. What would one not give, gentlemen of the jury, for the opportunity to examine the man who led the great expedition against Troy, or Odysseus, or Sisyphus, and innumerable other men and women one could mention? It would be an extraordinary happiness to talk with them, to keep company with them and examine them. In any case, they would certainly not put one to death for doing so. They are happier there than we are here in other respects, and for the rest of time they are deathless, if indeed what we are told is true. (Plato, c. 360 B.C.E./1997b, 41b–41c)

The day before the trial began, the Athenians sent a ship to Delos, part of a ritual in honor of Apollo. While the ship was away, there was a moratorium on executions. So Socrates lived another month in captivity. His friends tried to persuade him to flee so that he could look after his family and continue his philosophical investigations. He refused to escape Athens, not believing that death was something to be feared, and submitted himself to the punishment, drinking the cup of hemlock with great dignity.

After his death, his reputation continued to grow. Some followers wrote dialogues, often proposing their own ideas through the mouth of Socrates. In Plato's dialogues, we see other traces of the great celebrity he enjoyed. People search out those who knew him or could recall or recite his conversation. Travelers come to Athens to plead that someone read a dialogue Socrates once had that later, after clarifications and corrections, was committed to parchment. One follower arrives in another town and is entreated earnestly to recite by memory a conversation he heard Socrates have with others. We see people traveling to ask someone to recite a dialogue he had heard from another person who had heard it from another person. Socrates was the teaching profession's first superstar, and has remained one for many centuries.

Chapter 2

HOW TO EXAMINE LIFE
The Two Socratic Methods

> Let me explain his method of reply where the disputant had no clear statement to make, but without attempt at proof chose to contend that such or such a person named by himself was wiser, or more of a statesman, or more courageous, and so forth, than some other person. Socrates had a way of bringing the whole discussion back to the underlying proposition, as thus:
>
> **Socrates:** You state that so and so, whom you admire, is a better citizen than this other whom I admire?
>
> **The Disputant:** Yes; I repeat the assertion.
>
> **Socrates:** But would it not have been better to inquire first what is the work or function of a good citizen?
>
> —Xenophon, *Memorabilia*

Two Socratic Methods

In reading Plato's dialogues, you see different approaches to teaching. For example, you see effective lectures and storytelling. Protagoras tells a story to explain how virtue can be taught in *Protagoras*; Socrates recounts the allegory of the Cave in *The Republic*. But Socrates is best known for his one-on-one examinations of other people. I will call this method of examination Socratic Method 1. It was used to accompany the other person in investigating and evaluating the premises, consistency, and consequences of a claim to knowledge. But in *Meno*, you see Socrates use a different method to guide a young man in solving a problem in geometry. This method of shared problem solving I will call Socratic Method 2.

What unites the two methods is the skillful use of inductive questioning. In this chapter, we will look at the two methods in more detail. Both can be applied to the sciences and humanities at any level of education.

Socratic Method 1

Socratic questioning is apparently very simple. In the writings of Xenophon and Plato, Socrates meets someone who makes a claim to knowledge and begins to ask questions about this claim. For example, he encounters Euthyphro, who is on his way to denounce his own father for murder, and claims to understand piety, his principal motivation for his action. Surprised at Euthyphro's intention and claim, Socrates asks the basic underlying question, "What is Piety?" (Plato, c. 398 B.C.E./1997e, 5a).

Euthyphro does not immediately articulate a definition, but instead gives examples of different pious actions. Socrates gently chides him that he did not ask for examples, but for the form that makes all actions pious. In modern terms, Socrates is leading Euthyphro to concept attainment. "What is Piety?" Euthyphro confidently answers, "Piety is what is loved by the gods" (Plato, c. 398 B.C.E./1997e, 6e). Socrates then begins an investigation of this answer.

Socrates guides the shared investigation through inductive questioning. He suggests analogies, examples, counterexamples, and applications. In this way, he embarks on an inductive cycle of analysis, application, and evaluation. In this process, both the questions and the answers are brief and incisive. Generally, Socrates seeks assent to a series of short statements that reveal the limitations and contradictions of the definition, which must therefore be rejected. Socrates, for example, asks Euthyphro whether the gods love unanimously, and he must confess they do not; some gods will love something that other gods hate. Because the gods are inconsistent in what they love, and therefore cannot be in agreement on what is pious, Euthyphro must suggest another definition, and this is examined in the same manner.

Typically Socrates and his acquaintance or friend will examine and reject several definitions of a concept, and in the end, they will not find a satisfactory one. Euthyphro must confront the reality that he really does not understand piety as clearly as he first believed. But he also grasps much better the real difficulties of what seemed at first to be a very obvious question. Perhaps too he has learned how to test his thinking. Figure 1 isolates the central elements of Socratic Method 1.

Socrates discerned the basic underlying concept at play in a discussion. In many dialogues, he would identify this concept, ask what it is, and, professing not to know the response, share an investigation of the possible answers. The concept was often a broad ethical or moral one with a variety of possible answers. Among the early dialogues, we see the questions in Figure 2.

The concept is not selected at random: It is important to the respondent. *functionally related.* In *Lysis*, for instance, two friends examine friendship; in *Laches*, two generals examine courage; and in *Protagoras*, Protagoras himself claims to be a teacher of virtue, and Socrates examines the nature of virtue and whether it is teachable. Clearly, it is important to Socrates that the concept have great personal meaning to the individual. In *Laches*, a figure says:

> You don't appear to me to know that whoever comes into close contact with Socrates and associates with him in conversation must necessarily, even if he began by conversing about something quite different in the first place, keep on being led by the man's arguments until he submits to answering questions about himself concerning both his present manner of life and the life he has lived hitherto. (Plato, c. 390 B.C.E./1997g, 187e)

Because the question was personally relevant, Socrates exacted the condition that the responses in the examination be completely sincere. The dialogue demands personal engagement and disclosure; it is not a verbal game of chess. In the *Gorgias*, he admonishes, "You're wrecking your earlier statements, Callicles, and you'd no longer be adequately inquiring into the truth of the matter with me if you speak contrary to what you think" (Plato, c. 385 B.C.E./1997f, 495a). In another dialogue, Protagoras wants to make a distinction simply for the sake of argument, and this greatly upsets Socrates, who exclaims,

> Don't do that to me! It's not this 'if you want' or 'if you agree' business I want to test. It's you and me I want to put on the

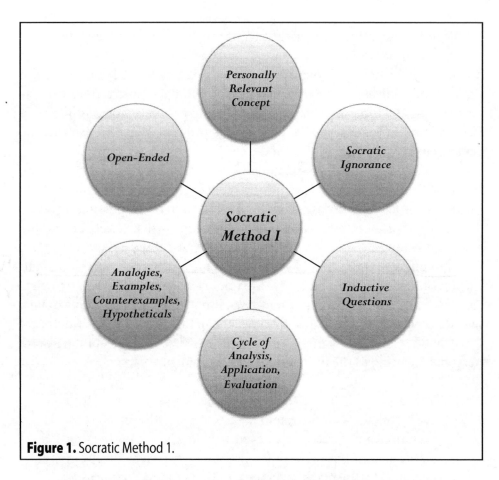

Figure 1. Socratic Method 1.

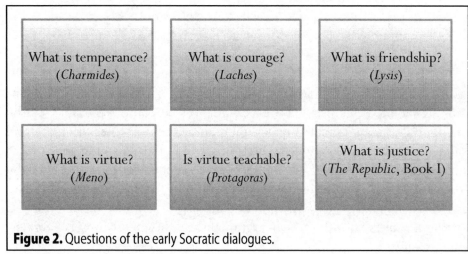

Figure 2. Questions of the early Socratic dialogues.

> line, and I think the argument will be tested best if we take the 'if' out. (Plato, c. 390 B.C.E./1997k, 331c)

The necessity of a personally relevant concept, and the insistence on personal engagement, make Socrates appear contemporary. Relevancy is a strong characteristic of authentic learning. Socrates wants to make authentic personal connections that lead to genuine understanding.

[handwritten margin note: Personal investment]

> **Socrates examined an apparently simple and personally relevant concept.**

Socratic Ignorance

Like all good teachers, Socrates did not give answers. In fact, Socrates denied knowledge of the answer! In *Apology*, Plato's version of the speech by Socrates during his trial, Socrates speaks at some length about his belief that he knows nothing. His one sliver of knowledge is that he is aware that he knows nothing. For this reason, he examines other men who claim to know something.

> So even now I continue this investigation as the god bade me—and I go around seeking out anyone, citizen or stranger, whom I think wise. Then if I do not think he is, I come to the assistance of the god and show him that he is not wise (Plato, c. 360 B.C.E./1997b, 23b)

[handwritten margin note: Do not give answers → leads to disengagement.]

Did he pretend not to know, or did he really not know? In various dialogues Socrates says that he really does not know. "I myself, Meno, am as poor as my fellow citizens in this matter, and I blame myself for my complete ignorance about virtue," he tells Meno (Plato, c. 380 B.C.E./1997i, 71b). To Critias, he says he does not know the answers to his own questions (Plato, c. 360 B.C.E./1997c, 165b–165c). At other times, however, he seems to express mock admiration, and an ironic tone is unmistakable. In any case, Socrates does not answer the fundamental question.

But as the questions advance, it becomes clear that Socrates has a very good idea of the limits of the other person's opinion. All the same, he does not come out and give an answer or make a declaration. This maintains and reinforces personal and active engagement. The other person cannot become passive and wait for the teacher to clarify the concept with a lecture, Socrates is the guide and facilitator, not the guru. The process of inductive questioning, the shared searching, becomes more important and indispensable. Through this, Socrates brings the person closer to an answer and teaches the method of investigation. Pedagogically, the denial of knowledge permits the shared and engaged exploration.

> **Socrates professed not to know the answer to the fundamental question.**

Inductive Questions and a Cycle of Analysis, Application, and Evaluation

Socrates moved the conversation in a clear and logical direction with inductive questions. Aristotle said that Socrates invented inductive reasoning, the reasoning from specific details to a general conclusion. Socrates began with what the other person knew and entered a cycle of analysis, application, and evaluation. He explains to Gorgias:

> I'm asking questions so that we can conduct an orderly discussion. It's not you I'm after; it's to prevent our getting in the habit of second-guessing and snatching each other's statements away ahead of time. It's to allow you to work out your assumption in any way you want. (Plato, c. 385 B.C.E./1997c, 454c)

By posing brief inductive questions, Socrates created clear, short steps that can be easily followed. He did not load a question with many subordinate clauses and conditions. He guided the discussion idea by idea. He made assumptions clear and pursued their implications and consequences. For example, let us look at a passage near the beginning of the *Alcibiades*.

Socrates: Then you are a good adviser about the things which you know?

Alcibiades: Certainly.

Socrates: And do you know anything but what you have learned of others, or found out yourself?

Alcibiades: That is all.

Socrates: And would you have ever learned or discovered anything, if you had not been willing either to learn of others or to examine yourself?

Alcibiades: I should not.

Socrates: And would you have been willing to learn or to examine what you supposed that you knew?

Alcibiades: Certainly not.

Socrates: Then there was a time when you thought that you did not know what you are now supposed to know?

Alcibiades: Certainly. (Plato, c. 390 B.C.E./1997a, 106d–106e)

Socrates soon elicits the subjects that Alcibiades has studied—writing, music, and wrestling—and brings him to realize that the Athenian Assembly has little use of advice in these subjects. And the topics that the Athenian Assembly does discuss—divination, city health, and shipbuilding, among others—are subjects about which Alcibiades knows very little. The Athenians will wish to listen carefully to experts regardless of social extraction, wealth, or beauty, the personal qualities about which the young Alcibiades is very proud and conceited.

Inductive questioning brings Alcibiades to a more honest assessment of his own capacities. As the conversation continues, Socrates brings Alcibiades to the awareness that he does not really understand what is just and unjust. At the same time, Socrates illuminates the general purpose of inductive questioning.

Socrates: But how are you ever likely to know the nature of justice and injustice, about which you are so perplexed, if you have neither learned them of others nor discovered them yourself?

Alcibiades: From what you say, I suppose not.

Socrates: See, again, how inaccurately you speak, Alcibiades!

Alcibiades: In what respect?

Socrates: In saying that I say so.

Alcibiades: Why, did you not say that I know nothing of the just and unjust?

Socrates: No; I did not.

Alcibiades: Did I, then?

Socrates: Yes.

Alcibiades: How was that?

Socrates: Let me explain. Suppose I were to ask you which is the greater number, two or one; you would reply "two"?

Alcibiades: I should.

Socrates: And by how much greater?

Alcibiades: By one.

Socrates: Which of us now says that two is more than one?

Alcibiades: I do.

Socrates: Did not I ask, and you answer the question?

Alcibiades: Yes.

Socrates: Then who is speaking? I who put the question, or you who answer me?

Alcibiades: I am.

Socrates: Or suppose that I ask and you tell me the letters which make up the name Socrates, which of us is the speaker?

Alcibiades: I am.

Socrates: Now let us put the case generally: whenever there is a question and answer, who is the speaker,—the questioner or the answerer?

Alcibiades: I should say, Socrates, that the answerer was the speaker.

Socrates: And have I not been the questioner all through?

Alcibiades: Yes.

Socrates: And you the answerer?

Alcibiades: Just so.

Socrates: Which of us, then, was the speaker?

Alcibiades: The inference is, Socrates, that I was the speaker.

Socrates: Did not someone say that Alcibiades, the fair son of Cleinias, not understanding about just and unjust, but thinking that he did understand, was going to the assembly to advise the Athenians about what he did not know? Was not that said?

Alcibiades: Very true.

Socrates: Then, Alcibiades, the result may be expressed in the language of Euripides. I think that you have heard all this "from yourself, and not from me"; nor did I say this, which you erroneously attribute to me, but you yourself, and what you said was very true. For indeed, my dear fellow, the design which you meditate of teaching what you do not know, and have not taken any pains to learn, is downright insanity. (Plato, c. 390 B.C.E./1997a, 112d–113c)

Socrates could have communicated the point he wanted to make with a short statement: "Alcibiades, you really do not know anything the Athenian Assembly needs to learn." But rather than do this, through questioning he establishes the premise that Alcibiades can only advise on what he knows, and then he inductively elicits what Alcibiades knows, and so demonstrates that the young man needs further study to contribute to the Athenian Assembly.

Questions lead Alcibiades to a greater awareness of the limits of his education. They bring him to greater self-knowledge. Is Socrates thinking for Alcibiades? In a sense, yes, but he begins with the statements offered by Alcibiades and reveals through a logical exploration their assumptions and implications.

Socrates asks many leading questions, that is, questions that suggest their own answers. In a courtroom, a lawyer relies on leading questions during cross examination, and studiously avoids open questions whose answers can depart in any direction and so potentially complicate the case. Leading questions control the witness. Typically in formulating a leading question, the lawyer makes a brief statement of a fact, avoiding any adverbs, and asks the witness to agree. *It was raining outside, wasn't it? You were wearing a black coat, correct?* Each question expresses one fact, and there can be no question about perception. Lawyers carefully plan and order the questions around a theme to reach a specific goal: to elicit helpful details or to impeach a witness. Their questions direct the testimony of the witness to a specific destination.

Did Socrates in a similar manner control his respondent in the agora? Yes and no. A contemporary lawyer is drawing out and assembling information helpful to his own legal argument. Socrates, on the other hand, was trying to investigate more analytically the premises, assumptions, and consequences of an argument. His leading questions permitted a controlled sequence of ideas. You can see the path an idea takes. The eminent British philosopher Gilbert Ryle (1966) said that these yes and no questions are essentially the Socratic Method.

The structure and sequence of the questioning is important. When Socrates refuted, there was a logical pattern to his questions (Vlastos, 1994). His partner in the investigation asserted a thesis and Socrates disagreed with it. The philosopher then gained agreement to other premises. He asserted that these new premises subvert or contradict the partner's first thesis. He claimed to have disproven the thesis. The respondent must then offer another.

In his questioning, Socrates often checked for understanding. There was always differentiation. If the other person did not understand, Socrates did not abruptly move on to another person or make a sarcastic remark (although at times he could be unkind, as Peter Geach demonstrated in a 1966 discussion of *Euthyphro*). He sought another path with other questions.

In *Laches*, for instance, the dialogue in which Socrates examines two generals for the definition of courage, Laches has difficulty in understanding the turn in discussion, but Socrates does not jump to another speaker (Plato, c. 390 B.C.E./1997g). He brings him forward with short statements, questions, and analogies, for as long as Laches wishes. In *Alcibiades*, when Alcibiades does understand how to answer a question, Socrates rephrases the question; he gives an example, he guides. He does not abandon the investigation (Plato, c. 390 B.C.E./1997a).

It is interesting to note too that Socrates was not the only one to ask questions. He was more than willing to have the answerer become the questioner. When Meno insists that Socrates answer his questions, Socrates consents willingly. What is important is the question and answer method, the shared logical exploration through analysis, application, and evaluation.

> **Socrates guided the person with inductive questions. There was a systematic cycle of analysis, application, and evaluation.**

Analogies, Examples, Counterexamples, Hypotheticals

Socrates guided his interlocutors through the use of analogies, examples, counterexamples, and hypothetical applications. He was famous for making references to occupations that everyone in Athens knew: doctors, athletic trainers, soldiers, sailors, cobblers. By grounding his references in daily life, he made his concepts more understandable.

Making analogies is one of the most creative acts of reasoning and remains important in many disciplines, from mathematics to science and from legal reasoning to political persuasion (Holyoak, 2005). With analogies, Socrates suggested similarities and clarified an idea. For instance, when Meno gives a definition of virtue that is too diffuse, saying there are many virtues according to the person, Socrates playfully suggests that Meno has offered a swarm, and he follows this quickly with an analogy taken from bees.

Socrates: But, Meno, to follow up the image of swarms, if I were asking you what is the nature of bees, and you said that they are many and of all kinds, what would you answer if I asked you: "Do you mean that they are many and varied and different from one another in so far as they are bees? Or are they no different in that regard, but in some other respect, in their beauty, for example, or their size or in some other such way?" Tell me, what would you answer if thus questioned?

Meno: I would say that they do not differ from one another in being bees.

Socrates: If I went on to say: "Tell me, what is this very thing, Meno, in which they are all the same and do not differ from one another?" Would you be able to tell me?

Meno: I would.

Socrates: The same is true in the case of the virtues. Even if they are many and various, all of them have one and the same form which makes them virtues, and it is right to look to this when one is asked to make clear what virtue is. Or do you not understand what I mean? (Plato, c. 380 B.C.E./1997i, 72b–72d)

What about in this situation?" [handwritten note]

Socrates used examples to teach his concepts and counterexamples as well as hypotheticals to refute an argument. A counterexample or hypothetical basically asks the question, *What about in this situation . . . ?* Counterexamples poured from Socrates. The great number itself is instructive. One counterexample alone is usually not enough to investigate or instruct. Socrates examined an idea by applying it to several other situations. For instance, when he investigates temperance (a notion that must be understood in its ancient Greek context), Charmides says that temperance is quietness, a kind of slow moderation. Socrates takes the definition and applies it to 11 different situations with virtually as many leading questions (Plato, c. 360 B.C.E./1997c). He goes through writing, reading, lyre-playing, boxing, running, and jumping, among other mental or physical activities that favor swiftness. All are activities that the young man would know, and so he can understand how his definition is lacking and must be modified in some way.

Examples were always taken from common life. Socrates tested ideas in the context of the experience of his respondents. People found themselves challenged to look at ideas in a novel way.

> **Socrates used analogies, examples, counterexamples, and hypotheticals to test and explore ideas.**

An Open Ending

Socrates, before I even met you I used to hear that you are always in a state of perplexity and that you bring others to the same state, and now I think you are bewitching and beguiling me, simply putting me under a spell, so that I am quite perplexed. Indeed, if a joke is in order, you seem, in appearance and in every other way, to be like the broad torpedo fish, for it too makes anyone who comes close and touches it feel numb, and you now seem to have had that kind of effect on me, for both my mind and my tongue are numb, and I have no answer to give you. (Plato, c. 380 B.C.E./1997i, 80a–80b)

Typically the so-called early dialogues are open-ended (although this is not true of the *Crito* and the *Gorgias*) and end with frustration; that is, Socrates and his respondents do not discover a final answer to the big question. What is more, the respondent often feels disoriented by this new awareness of ignorance. Several are not grateful for their shared investigation: Euthyphro hastily departs; Callicles becomes furious.

Does this mean that Socrates was a bad teacher?

On the contrary, in these open endings you see the greatness of Socrates as a teacher in his deep respect for the other person. A couple of ideas should be borne in mind. For Socrates, becoming aware of one's ignorance was an important step to clarifying one's ideas. If the respondents finish the dialogue without a clear solution, the reality is that they actually began the dialogue in confusion but were unaware of it. They believed they understood something they did not really understand. "Do you think," he asks Meno, "that before [the slave boy] would have tried to find out that which he thought he knew though he did not, before he fell into perplexity and realized he did not know and longed to know?" (Plato, c. 380 B.C.E./1997i, 84c). Through the process of questioning, Socrates brought the confusion to light.

More importantly, Socrates was not teaching an answer, he was teaching the method of investigation itself. In the same way that he multiplied examples to elicit a concept, the repetition of the inductive process of examining and discarding definitions inculcated the process of critical thinking. Socrates trained young Athenians to think: " . . . [the young men] themselves often imitate me and try to question others. I think they find an abundance of men who believe they have some knowledge but know little or nothing" (Plato, c. 360 B.C.E./1997b, 23d).

open ended questions!

Discussions often were open-ended.

Socrates and His Method

Some of the dialogues show Socrates refuting his respondent; others show him more constructively assisting in the articulation of an argument. In one passage he refers to this work as midwifery; that is, he helps others to give birth to their ideas (Plato, c. 355 B.C.E./1997m). The Socratic Method then can be used to dismantle faulty thinking and to lead the respondent to more correct and consistent thinking about a concept.

[handwritten: analogy to midwifery]

Let us review the points we have made:

- ✍ Socrates examined an apparently simple and fundamental moral concept that was personally important to the respondent.
- ✍ He professed not to know the answer.
- ✍ He guided the person with inductive questions.
- ✍ There was a systematic cycle of analysis, application, and evaluation.
- ✍ He used analogies, examples, counterexamples, and hypothetical situations to explore ideas.
- ✍ Discussions often were open-ended.

These are the six major characteristics of the first Socratic method, and they mix and manifest themselves differently in the varied dialogues of Plato. Socrates was not lecturing and then testing for information—he was instructing the other person in how to think about a concept, how to examine different points of view. He taught a shared method of critical thinking. Thinking critically was a social activity, not a solitary exercise.

[handwritten: critical thinking is a social activity]

The Socratic Method is not one of its characteristics in isolation. It is not, for instance, the use of leading questions or arguing through examples and counterexamples. It is not simply having a conversation, an interview, or a dialogue. It is all of the characteristics used dynamically and differentiated according to the concept and the person. Through this method, Socrates inductively guided others to discovery and self-knowledge.

You can also recognize crucial elements of the modern scientific method. There is no argument from authority, but instead an attitude of skepticism. You make observations or suggest a hypothesis, design an experiment (application), analyze data, and then make an evaluation. There is inductive reasoning and an open ending, for any scientific theory or explanation is not proven right, it is simply not proven wrong. Science continually refines itself in a most Socratic manner. If Socrates brought philosophy down from the heavens, as Cicero said, scientists later refined and brought his method back to the heavens.

Now, how can we apply Bloom's revised taxonomy to this first Socratic method? We can place the instruction of Socrates in the categories of higher level thinking. He is applying, analyzing, and evaluating, and through this he is creating. The analogy of the midwife best represents the positive character of the Socratic Method.

Socratic Method 2

The second form of the Socratic Method is a guided inquiry leading to the correct understanding of a problem, and then following a process to obtain a correct answer. In the well-known teaching format *I do, We do, You do*, the second form of the Socratic Method begins with problem solving in the middle phase, *We do*: Socrates and his partner together reasoned through the process of problem solving. For Plato, this demonstrated a doctrine of knowledge as recollection. Today the intention is to construct the bridge from *We do* to *You do*; that is, from teacher-assisted solving of the problem to autonomous solving.

In the *Meno*, Socrates meets his young friend, whose name titles the dialogue and who is a student of the sophist Gorgias. The two begin a discussion about what virtue is. After a few attempts, Meno is at a loss to define it. But, acknowledging Socrates' profession of ignorance, Meno does not understand how Socrates can recognize a correct answer, and asks,

> How will you look for it, Socrates, when you do not know at all what it is? How will you aim to search for something you do not know at all? If you should meet with it, how will you know that this is the thing that you did not know? (Plato, c. 380 B.C.E./1997i, 80d)

To answer these questions, Socrates tells a story that proposes that knowledge is innate, that we are born knowing certain ideas, and that education is the process of eliciting this knowledge. Knowing is remembering. He then demonstrates this theory by examining a slave boy on a problem of geometry: how to double the area of a square (see Figure 3). At first, the slave boy suggests two solutions that prove incorrect. But Socrates takes another tact:

Socrates: Look then how he will come out of his perplexity while searching along with me. I shall do nothing more than ask questions and not teach him. Watch

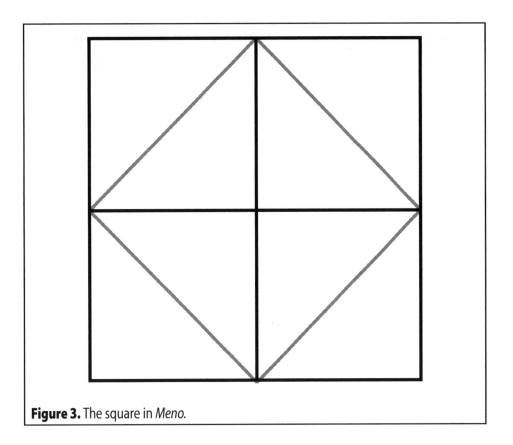

Figure 3. The square in *Meno*.

whether you find me teaching and explaining things to him instead of asking for his opinion.

You tell me, is this not a four-foot figure? You understand?

Boy: I do.

Socrates: We add to it this figure which is equal to it?

Boy: Yes.

Socrates: And we add this third figure equal to each of them?

Boy: Yes.

Socrates: Could we then fill in the space in the corner?

Boy: Certainly.

Socrates: So we have these four equal figures?

Boy: Yes.

Socrates: Well then, how many times is the whole figure larger than this one?

Boy: Four times.

Socrates: But we should have had one that was twice as large, or do you not remember?

Boy: I certainly do.

Socrates: Does not this line from one corner to the other cut each of these figures in two?

Boy: Yes.

Socrates: So these are four equal lines which enclose this figure?

Boy: They are.

Socrates: Consider now: how large is the figure?

Boy: I do not understand.

Socrates: Within these four figures, each line cuts off half of each, does it not?

Boy: Yes.

Socrates: How many of this size are there in this figure?

Boy: Four.

Socrates: How many in this?

Boy: Two.

Socrates: What is the relation of four to two?

Boy: Double.

Socrates: How many feet in this?

Boy: Eight.

Socrates: Based on what line?

Boy: This one.

Socrates: That is, on the line that stretches from corner to corner of the four-foot figure?

Boy: Yes.

Socrates: Clever men call this the diagonal, so that if diagonal is its name, you say that the double figure would be that based on the diagonal?

Boy: Most certainly, Socrates.

Socrates: What do you think, Meno? Has he, in his answers, expressed any opinion that was not his own?

Meno: No, they were all his own.

Socrates: And yet, as we said a short time ago, he did not know?

Meno: That is true. (Plato, c. 380 B.C.E./1997i, 84d–85c)

Although the theory of innate knowledge remains fascinating, and we could go further in discussing other aspects of this dialogue (e.g., the role of hypothesis), we will look at the method used to elicit the correct understanding. Its elements are:

- a problem,
- Socratic ignorance,
- inductive questions,
- alternatives for exploration,
- diagrams, and
- a solution.

These elements are immediately applicable to problem solving in general. Note that Socrates is not drilling the slave in the process (which is not to say that drilling does not have a role in education). He is helping him to discover the answer on his own. A more recent and very enjoyable classic of this second Socratic method, and one that elaborates and explains it further, is *How to Solve It* (1945/1957) by George Pólya. Many teachers today might not accompany a student, as Socrates does, in following a process to an erroneous answer. The effort to guide to a correct response would be present from the beginning.

The Two Socratic Methods

These elements of the two basic methods of Socrates in the dialogues of Plato can be combined to become a constructive exploration of an idea. Together, the two methods develop the skills most needed for 21st-century learning, critical thinking, and problem solving.

What is also striking is that the dialogues of Plato manifest the methods mixed in many different ways; that is, there is considerable freedom in teaching through the Socratic Method, whatever allowances we rightly make for the literary nature of the dialogues. In *Meno*, for instance, we see Method I (the discussion of virtue) linked to Method II (the problem of geometry). We see Socrates engaging Meno in an examination of virtue through questions and answers, we see Meno put Socrates on the spot to elaborate with more clarity, and then Socrates leads the slave boy through a problem of geometry. In other dialogues, however, we see Method I combined with minilectures, citations of poetry, and the creation of profound myths in order to bring a rich panoply of ideas into play. The Socratic Method is one of many tools for instruction in the dialogues.

Although you can rightfully praise Plato for his sophisticated literary genius, and demonstrate this in great complexity, and declare that such myth-spinning and minilectures were not in the teaching toolkit of the original Socrates who conversed in the cobbler's shop, the point in the end is that many dialogues, except perhaps those that become monotonously essayistic, are rich teaching experiences, often modeling the variety and pacing of effective teachers in the classroom.

Socrates denied being a teacher, yet he facilitated learning in a remarkable manner. Plato very clearly was a teacher as well and continues to be one. He shows us the shared inductive examination of concepts, the probing of ambiguities, the trial and error investigation of problems, all through sophisticated questioning on the plane of higher level thinking.

Chapter 3

BE CAREFUL WHAT YOU ASK FOR
Preparing a Socratic Dialogue

> So we got up and walked around the courtyard. I wanted to see what Hippocrates was made of, so I started to examine him with a few questions.
>
> —Plato, *Gorgias*

For Socrates, the question-and-answer dialogue was a shared method for examining moral questions. Often he was refuting the claim of the other person. In other dialogues, rather than only dismantling inadequate claims and arguments, Socrates became the midwife who helped the other person give birth to his idea. Similarly, in the classroom, one can use Socratic dialogue to clarify, frame, challenge, and extend student thinking. It guides slow thinking about claims, concepts, issues, and problems of all kinds.

It is not always possible in school, but if we were to imitate Socrates closely, we would establish the content of our dialogues by the issues suggested by the students themselves. The personally relevant issue was the starting point for Socrates, and his aim was the increase of self-knowledge. In the 1960s and 1970s, there were advocates of negotiating the syllabus more along these lines (e.g., Postman & Weingartner, 1969; Stanford, 1977). Today, democratic schools such as Sudbury Valley School in Massachusetts more radically continue this policy. But typical middle school and high school curricula do provide many issues that are personally relevant to the students, and they prepare them to participate in society by entering the workforce or continuing their education. In the middle and high school curricula of the sciences and the humanities, you can find many opportunities for both Socratic methods.

Socratic dialogue also was differentiated to an individual. In effect, it was a one-on-one tutoring session. In the contemporary classroom, often it is more difficult, but not impossible, to teach students in this way. Nonetheless, making the necessary concessions for the contemporary classroom, the Socratic Method permits the meticulous examination of claims, concepts, issues, and problems. It is an effective and flexible method of discovery learning for middle and high school students.

You can distinguish three broad objectives in pursuing a Socratic dialogue. First, as in the *Meno*, you can accompany the student in solving a problem or following a procedure. Secondly, as in the early Socratic dialogues, you can clarify, analyze, and evaluate a concept. Lastly, imitating Socrates the midwife, you can creatively bring an idea to life, not for refutation, but by defining it and then exploring its assumptions, implications, and consequences. These three forms of dialogue can be combined in countless ways to probe and examine claims, issues, and problems in a logical and creative manner.

The most challenging aspect of all three variations, I believe, is the one most often dropped from adaptations, namely, the inductive sequence. In its stricter form, the Socratic Method is not an open discussion, an interview, a rote recitation, or a controlled debate. A series of open questions, or a clash of opinions, is not the Socratic Method. In a Socratic dialogue, there is a more careful analysis of an argument, moving inductively from premise to premise to a conclusion or generalization. A Socratic dialogue possesses the strengths and weaknesses of induction. To engage another person in this fluid examination is the challenge.

The beginning point for this investigation is what the students think. You must clearly understand what the students think regarding the concept. The best way is to ask them, as Socrates did. This can be done at the beginning of class if the concept is not very complex. Otherwise, survey the students for their ideas on the Preparation Sheet (see page 140), then read and reflect on the answers, looking for patterns or common features, before planning the examination. If you do not know where they are, you cannot explore what they think, and you cannot guide them to the destination.

Keeping clearly in mind that the dialogue in the classroom will make any necessary adaptation to further student understanding, and that student responses may alter its direction, we will look at how to plan and outline a dialogue. First, we will look at Socratic Method 1, which addresses the analysis and evaluation of a concept. Then, we will briefly look at Socratic Method 2, which guides the student through a problem in a set process, not

[Handwritten margin note: Beginning point is asking them what they think - ASK! (Don't assume)]

as a drill, but accompanying the student to more autonomous performance in the process.

In learning how to prepare and conduct a Socratic dialogue, and to familiarize the students gradually with its elements and dynamics, first organize short dialogues about 5 minutes in length aimed at concept attainment. From this, you can understand the inductive dynamics and begin to construct longer dialogues.

The Dialogue Binder

For preparation, you can use a notebook or computer, but a Dialogue Binder keeps materials organized better for reference and use. The organization of the Dialogue Binder is chiefly by concept, issue, or problem. Large tabs flag these sections. Within these sections, six smaller tabs mark teaching objectives, definitions, brainstorming, research, inductive question outlines, and teaching reflections.

Socratic Method 1: Concept Analysis and Evaluation

The Socratic analysis and evaluation of a concept is demanding to prepare. What is most crucial is to understand the concept thoroughly, where misunderstanding can occur, the appropriate inductive sequence of questions, and how understanding can be extended. What makes it demanding, and very worthwhile, is that the concepts often are multifaceted, and multidimensional. There is not necessarily one correct answer, but one answer can be more correct than another. In more sophisticated dialogues, you probe the ambiguities of the concept, its application, and evaluation.

To begin, what are the objectives? The objectives determine the elements and structure of the dialogue. Clarifying the specific aims for yourself and your students gives a direct line of vision to their attainment. Bloom's revised taxonomy, as we discussed in the Introduction, allows you to articulate precise goals.

You can select a single objective or combine them. Socratic Method 1, however, is anchored (but entirely restricted to) Conceptual Knowledge. Socrates explored concepts such as piety and justice. He defined, applied, analyzed, and evaluated. Dialogues in Socratic Method 1 are in this same cycle.

Form follows function in Socratic dialogues. The objectives of the dialogue immediately suggest the elements and structure the dialogue will have. For example, concept attainment (a good place to begin) will inevitably have examples and counterexamples that must be inductively classified and explained. The application of a rule or principle will have hypothetical situations, leading often to challenging ambiguities, gray areas that require greater refinement in making distinctions and establishing priorities. Analysis will require the lucid breaking down of the situation or problem into its pieces, laying bare their relationships. Evaluation requires the application of criteria for judgment. Connections to previously covered curriculum require memory questions. All of these operations can be approached inductively. With the objectives defined, the shape of the dialogue begins to appear.

You must decide approximately how much time the dialogue will require in the classroom. Here there is much latitude, for the dialogue can be 5 minutes or 50 minutes; it can be strictly Socratic for the entire duration, or have one phase of a discussion in another format. For instance, you can prepare a more open discussion on a text, but during this open discussion enter a phase in which you clarify, analyze, and evaluate a key concept in a more rigorously Socratic way. Then, make a transition back to open discussion. In reading the dialogues of Plato, you see that the Socratic conversations in reality were not simply a series of questions and answers. Participants made more extended reflections, recounted fables, and even delivered interesting and cogent minilectures and longer speeches. Socratic questioning can be comfortably and appropriately placed as a phase in a broader discussion. It can be inserted in any place of the lesson plan where concept attainment and careful analysis are necessary.

Record the objectives and the time required in the Dialogue Binder.

Three Steps

There are then three steps in preparation:
1. Select and define a concept.
2. Brainstorm: Research—begin the inductive outline.
3. Complete the inductive outline.

Step 1: Select and Define a Concept

Socrates examined claims, concepts, and issues that were deeply important to the people with whom he conversed. There was a dramatic event, an important decision, a pressing issue or argument whose central claim or concept needed to be clarified, analyzed, evaluated, and understood. The personally relevant concept will be most easily found in situations that impact the students directly. The first step for a classroom dialogue is to select or discover such a concept within the curriculum.

What are worthwhile concepts for the middle school or high school classroom? In science, for instance, the concepts would include anything from hypothesis or theory to larger concepts of matter, energy, light, space, motion, and force. Themes in literary or artistic works in the curriculum suggest concepts, as will many different primary sources in social studies or history classes. In many classes, the concepts will be from the textbook or a specific text, but one can also select a concept without a text; for example, one can examine the concept of freedom. One can also compare and contrast concepts that are in tension (e.g., realpolitik and global citizenship, or Neoclassical and Romantic styles).

For further suggestions, Mortimer Adler (1984b), the indefatigable popularizer of philosophy and advocate of the Great Books, isolated about 100 concepts for reflection and discussion, although he later pruned the list in other publications. The list in Figure 4 is based on his excellent list, but I have subtracted a few concepts and added others. Of course the list is not exhaustive, and is intended only for suggestions, but it would be more than sufficient for many semesters!

Define the concept very clearly. You can use a dictionary for this, but rich concepts have different facets; that is, they have a set of varied ideas clustered around them. It is necessary to see these facets and the directions in which they lead. A regular dictionary will be a beginning, but more specialized resources will be necessary to consult to understand the concept in greater, more appropriate depth.

Definitions in reality can be very challenging, and take three forms. You can define with a synonym, a word with nearly the same meaning; or with an example, which is a representative instance; or you can formulate an analytic definition, a short and precise description of the most important characteristics. All three forms will be helpful, for often there can be disagreement on what the appropriate definition is, which precisely was what Socrates made evident. Write these core ideas for the concept in your Dialogue Binder. They will be expanded and elaborated in the next step.

[Handwritten margin note: Define by 1. synonym 2. example 3. analytic definition]

Animal	Matter
Art	Memory
Artificial Intelligence	Mind
Beauty	Nationalism
Cause	Nature
Chance	Opinion
Change	Pleasure
Citizen	Poetry
Constitution	Progress
Democracy	Punishment
Desire	Realpolitik
Duty	Reasoning
Education	Relation
Emotion	Relativism
Equality	Religion
Evolution	Revolution
Experience	Right
Family	Sense
Free Market	Sin
Friendship	Singularity
Global Citizenship	Slavery
God	Social Contract
Good And Evil	Socialism
Government	Soul
Habit	Space
Happiness	State
Honor	Sustainable Development
Human	Technology
Imagination	Time
Imperialism	Truth
Intuition	Tyranny
Judgment	Utilitarianism
Justice	Violence
Knowledge	Virtue And Vice
Labor	War And Peace
Law	Wealth
Liberty (Or Freedom)	Wisdom
Life And Death	World
Love	

Figure 4. Suggestions for concepts for analysis and discussion.

Now you have recorded in the Dialogue Binder the objectives, the time required, and the concept for exploration, as well as its definition(s). The order in which these are clarified does not matter as much as their clarification. At the outset, you might know that in teaching the Declaration of Independence, for example, you will investigate the concepts of equality, rights, life, liberty, and happiness. But you will have to establish how much time the schedule permits for Socratic investigation. You may have to prioritize and make choices in terms of length of coverage, devoting more time to equality and happiness without unduly neglecting the other three concepts. You cannot introduce and thoroughly understand such profound concepts in a single class session.

Step 2: Brainstorm: Research—Begin the Inductive Outline

In reading the dialogues of Plato, I marvel at the agility of Socrates in understanding the nature, the assumptions, the limits, and the consequences of ideas. In planning a dialogue for the classroom, it is important for the teacher to understand the concept as completely as possible. This does not mean that every possible angle is understood—this really is never the case with open-ended concepts—but you should be familiar with the core ideas, the fundamental lines and turns, and the basic assumptions and common consequences.

So after defining the concept, you must research more thoroughly. This will send you to the Internet as well as to the reference section of the library.

To canvas a rich concept is challenging. Definitions can be protean, changing in different contexts and historical periods, and you must unfailingly keep the discussion relevant to the middle school or high school classroom, not a university lecture hall. Often, important concepts are influencing each other. For example, equality is difficult to consider in isolation from justice or fairness. You will need to understand the borders, or overlapping areas, or levels of the concept.

A philosophical dictionary or encyclopedia will always be helpful to consult, but you sometimes will have to work to bring the ideas to daily language. An excellent online resource, but one which delves deeply, is *The Stanford Encyclopedia of Philosophy* (http://plato.stanford.edu). Another valuable and more concise resource is *The Oxford Companion to Philosophy* (Honderich, 1995). The works of Bryan Magee (1998), Nigel Warburton (2004), Stephen Law (2003, 2007), and Julian Baggini (2002; Baggini & Fosl, 2010) are admirably lucid and present the essential ideas on many key concepts, as well as signposts to further reading. You will not find all of the concepts listed in Figure 4 in a single resource.

The further removed the concept is from the student's experience, personal or educational, the more difficult it is to teach. The unfamiliar concept begins as an abstraction, and bringing it into the student's reach is more difficult. If the examples are unfamiliar to the students, they have no steps to ascend, and more information is needed before you can pursue analysis and evaluation. Socratic questioning is not for imparting information, but for thinking about what you know.

no more than 7 key bullet points

Now, write in the Dialogue Binder in bullet points exactly what the students should understand. These key ideas should be limited in number, no more than seven. A very short dialogue, perhaps a phase within a larger discussion, might have just one key idea that will be meticulously examined, explored, and evaluated. A simple concept attainment dialogue may just arrive at one key idea. In learning how to question inductively, one point is sufficient. Once confidence has been achieved, three to five points work very well. These bullet points make the dialogue goal-oriented. They are the destinations for the inductive journey.

The next task, which has its own section in the Dialogue Binder, is to begin an inductive outline leading to these points. Generally, we use outlines that begin with a heading and then list points and subpoints below. As Craddock (2001) observed, an inductive outline flows in the opposite direction, for induction moves from particular observations to generalizations. Subpoints lead to points, points lead to headings, which are generalizations or conclusions. The inductive outline is organized backward; the destinations are known and become the discoveries of the students.

Inductive outline is backwards

The bullet points you have written down become the headings of the outline. The task now is to guide the students to these headings through questions, analogies, examples, counterexamples, and hypotheticals. The inductive path should be direct and unambiguous. The aim is not "by indirections find directions out." A serpentine Socratic path is frustrating to follow, and so try to survey the straightest path possible to the destination.

Step 3: Complete the Inductive Outline

Socrates taught through systematic exploration and discovery. His discussions did not wander through topics in free association. Systematic questions give structure to a Socratic discussion. The appropriate content and sequence is determined by the headings established in the previous step. Now, draft in the Dialogue Binder an outline of inductive questions—using analogies, examples, counterexamples, and hypotheticals, as well as other inductive questions—that has a well-defined introduction, development, and conclusion.

Introduction to the Dialogue

The introduction must hook the students, and you must understand where it leaves you. It can take many effective and dramatic forms, eliciting why the concept is important as well as making clear what the students think. Often it will be productive to distribute the opening question on a preparation sheet a few days before the dialogue, to allow more reflection.

Knowing what the students think is fundamentally important. You can then envision the direction and length of the bridge to the concept, conclusion, or generalization you have designated as the destination. Surveying opinion is not the Socratic Method, but it makes clear the starting point from which the journey begins. Your introduction should be chosen with this in mind.

Here are four ways of opening a dialogue concerning the concept of revolution.

1. **A dramatic anecdote and a question.** Stories are excellent teaching tools that never go out of style. Select one that introduces the concept or relates analogously to it.
   a. Example: On April 3, 1973, John F. Mitchell and Dr. Martin Cooper demonstrated the first mobile phone. Made by Motorola, it weighed 2.2 pounds. Ten years later, it became possible to buy mobile phones. In 1984, the Motorola DynaTAC 8000X, the first commercially available mobile phone, cost nearly $4,000 and allowed you to talk for 30 minutes. (Show the picture of the phone.) Was this revolution in communication quick or slow? What provoked it?

2. **An open question.** An open question that has been shared beforehand with the students stimulates lively discussion on the concept. Students understand their own opinions better with preparation. You want an answer that may begin, "It depends . . ."
   a. Example: Is gradual change (evolution) better than drastic and quick change (revolution)?

3. **A controversial quotation.** Controversy sparks lively discussion (Brookfield & Preskill, p. 71). Reading a quotation that bluntly expresses an opinion will provoke a strong response with ideas for analysis.
   a. Example: "Are the people calling for true justice? Instead of that we'll give them a justice that is just a bit less unjust . . . They want revolution . . . ? We give them reforms . . . reforms by the bucketful . . . we'll drown them with reforms . . . or rather we'll

[handwritten margin notes: 1) Story & Question 2) Open Q 3) Controversial Q 4) Dilemma]

drown them with promises of reforms, because we'll never going to give them reforms either!" (Fo, 1992, pp.195–196)

4. **A dilemma.** Present a dilemma with the issue in the center.

   a. Example: A cruel dictator rules a country that has stability and a reasonable level of prosperity. If the dictator is overthrown, there may be bitter fighting between political and religious factions. Is it better to rebel and overthrow the dictator, perhaps igniting a civil war, or should the population wait for more gradual political change?

Development of the Inductive Outline

In Step 2, you articulated key ideas that became the headings for exploration in the dialogue. Now, the task is to create the paths that achieve the aims of the dialogue. The inductive sequence is one of the most distinguishing features of the Socratic Method. You must continue and finish brainstorming for the questions, examples, counterexamples, hypotheticals, and analogies that will guide the students. After this, you must review and reflect on an effective sequence, then build an orderly series of steps to the key ideas.

There are myriad ways of brainstorming. You can create a concept map, or simply list ideas, or record them in a flow chart. Or you can divide the paper into five sections marked *Questions, Analogies, Examples, Counterexamples, Hypotheticals*. You can simply begin to write questions (knowing much revision will be done).

My personal preference is for concept mapping. Invented by Joseph D. Novak in the 1970s, the concept map visually represents the big picture of what must be understood (Novak & Gowin, 1984). This concept map in turn can be pruned and clarified to become a graphic organizer for the students, if more scaffolding is desired.

Questions have a variety of roles. In general, they should be short statements seeking assent and drawn out statements (i.e., premises) that lead inductively to conclusions. In *Alcibiades*, for instance, Socrates at the outset draws a series of premises from young Alcibiades regarding knowledge. These in turn become the foil against which to test the reality of the young man's knowledge. In the terms of Bloom's taxonomy, questions can also guide the essential procedures of application, analysis, and evaluation. They can solicit facts (fact questions are not banished from Socratic dialogue, but cannot dominate) and assess understanding by asking students to paraphrase or restate. They can pivot the discussion to consideration of alternative views.

Leading questions are unpopular with many teachers, but they do have a place in Socratic pedagogy. They may be used as small steps to bring out statements and inferences in more intricate reasoning. It requires incisive understanding to phrase precisely the questions that guide the student to analysis and evaluation, as Edward Warren (1942) remarked.

Analogies are an important part of reasoning in the works of Plato. They introduce, clarify, or further explain an idea; they can also move an argument forward. As I mentioned earlier, they continue to be fundamentally important in teaching mathematics, science, and many other subjects at all levels of education (Holyoak, 2005; Newby, Ertmer, & Stepich, 1995). Analogies are also the comparisons made in metaphors and similes in poetry and literature read at all ages. Elementary school children learn about analogies. Middle school and high school children learn the power of analogies. At university they can be used effectively. Richard Feynman, one of the most gifted teachers of the 20th century as well as a Nobel Prize winning physicist, constantly made imaginative and memorable analogies in his lectures at CalTech to instill an understanding of physics. The Miller Analogies Test (MAT), which solely consists of 120 analogies, is used today as a standard form of assessment for entrance to many graduate schools (Zahler, 2010).

Analogies make comparisons and suggest relationships between objects, concepts, or processes. The familiar object, concept, or process is called the *source* or *analogue*; the unfamiliar object, concept, or process to be explained or understood is called the *target*. Usually there is a connecting word (*like* or *as* or another expression) and, in a classroom setting, an explanation of the similarity or dissimilarity. The form of parallel reasoning may be stated as *A is related to B in the same way as C is related to D*. In briefest terms, which is helpful to know for brainstorming or note-making, the analogy may be expressed as a ratio—pine : tree :: seagull : bird.

Analogies are the teacher's best friend. They are extraordinarily versatile elements of the Socratic dialogue. They can be inserted anywhere to clarify a concept, a word, or a process. Some of the common relationships expressed in analogies follow.

- synonyms,
- antonyms,
- degree of intensity,
- classification,
- part/whole,
- conversion of terms,
- characteristic,
- sequence,
- object/action, and
- worker/product (Wormeli, 2009; Zahler, 2010)

Mapping analogies requires selecting a source familiar to the students and then choosing the characteristics to be mapped to the target. For the classroom, the best analogies are from the personal experiences of the students. Discovering an appropriate analogy is a eureka moment. Rick Wormeli (2009) made the excellent suggestion of surveying the students for their background in travel, family, and specific interests. Memorable analogies are also readily found in fairy tales, fables, children's stories, games, sports, song lyrics, novels, or a recent event in the news. Brainstorming requires listing sources familiar to the students and their characteristics, then seeking connections with the target area.

For example, in speaking about the concept of liberty, one may define it as the absence of coercion (Warburton, 2004). A person at liberty is not being forced to things he or she does not wish to do. This freedom extends to the point where someone else is harmed by our actions. In terms of an analogy, we can look at baseball. If you have the equipment and know how to play, you are free to play baseball until you throw a reckless pitch or charge the mound or throw the bat or do something else that could hurt someone. Then you will be ejected from the game. You are coerced to leave because you have intentionally hurt someone.

For another example, a rival concept of liberty is the freedom to control your own life. You are not simply free from coercion; you are empowered to participate to the fullness of your potential and desire. Should a state ensure that all of its members have this sort of freedom? In terms of the baseball analogy, should the state ensure that everyone has the same equipment and learns how to play the game? Should it ensure that anyone can learn and develop their potential in any desired sport?

In an argument, analogies suggest that the similarity or dissimilarity between two things or processes makes a conclusion probable (but not certain!). Analogies are persuasive, but can oversimplify or overgeneralize. Students learn to distinguish between *strong analogies* whose comparisons share similarities and *weak analogies* whose comparisons and contrasts are fewer and less cogent. In dialogues, they should make the point quickly and you should check for understanding.

Examples and counterexamples can have various roles. First, they can be simple illustrations, as you see in dictionaries. For instance, we define the word *tyrant* as one who exercises power in a vicious and arbitrary way. In the world of fiction, examples would be Lord Voldemort in the Harry Potter stories, the White Witch in *The Lion, the Witch, and the Wardrobe*, and Sauron in the Lord of the Rings trilogy. In the real world, an example would be Saddam Hussein.

Secondly, examples may be collected and presented in series to define the concept inductively. In a very basic way, this is the strategy of concept attainment, which presents positive and negative instances of a concept, and students compare and contrast to discern the concept (Johnson, Carlson, Kastl, & Kastl, 1992). For simpler ideas, this is straightforward. Examples of toys and tools, nouns and proper nouns, prime numbers and composite numbers can be differentiated. For more abstract concepts, this can be more difficult in some cases. But, as if one flipped the dictionary definition, one leads to the concept by a series of examples: What do Lord Voldemort, the White Witch, and Sauron have in common?

Thirdly and similarly, examples can present cases that become an inductive argument for a conclusion. For instance, in addressing the question of political rights, and specifically, whether a young person should be able to vote at age 16, what are other examples of civil responsibilities that may be carried by young people?

- Young people can begin to drive at 16.
- From the age of 14, teens can begin to work (with restrictions) for wages and pay federal income taxes and social security. From the age of 16, there are fewer restrictions on work.
- With parental and/or judicial consent, in many states teens can get married at 16.
- Scotland will allow young people of 16 to vote in their national independence referendum in 2014.
- Austria allows young people to vote at 16.

Conclusion: From the age of 16, many young people can drive, work, pay taxes, and social security, and get married. Could our states consider allowing young people to vote?

The best examples will avoid clichés, not be recondite, and be taken from the experience and education of the students. One can move outward from that experience or, beginning with more remote examples, toward it. Moving from the concrete to the abstract is always more effective.

Counterexamples also constrain the student to examine another point of view, a counterargument. They can often be used in response to examples elicited from the students. The aim is not to halt the student's line of reasoning, but to pose the follow-up question of why or how the counterexample forces a reconsideration or refinement. This allows the students to reflect on the reasoning involved. Students should also be encouraged to make the inductive counterargument against you (more on this in the next chapter). Examples and counterexamples can also be spontaneously solicited from the students in the classroom. At times, it may be helpful to derive the counterexamples from a single contrasting concept. For example, in examining revolution, contrast the concept with counterexamples from evolution.

How one handles an alternative viewpoint or a counterargument is very important. It should be strongly and clearly stated and developed, not watered down and weakened. There should be no rhetorical sleight of hand to make ideas vanish. What is the other side of the concept, issue, or problem? How does the counterargument develop inductively? What would be the counteranalogy and counterexample? How does it compare and contrast with the argument or other viewpoints?

Hypotheticals are the "What if?" questions, which can be phrased in many ways, that apply the concept to different projected situations or alter significant variables in the same situation. They are an effective way of understanding the implications of a concept (or rule, principle, decision, or assumption) or a specific variable. The hypothetical should be one clear sentence unburdened with qualifying clauses. It should not be complex paragraph-long problems whose details are difficult to absorb by the listener (remember, this is an oral exercise). In their brevity, hypotheticals are higher level questions that ask students to make quick judgments. They are small thought experiments. They can be used singly, or they can be extended and sequenced for inductive exploration.

By organizing hypotheticals in a carefully calibrated inductive series, you can test the concept (Katz & O'Neill, 2009). For instance, you alter a variable in the situation, so the series incrementally tests the impact of that variable. As the variable alters, what happens to the concept (or rule, principle, decision, or assumption)? Does it eventually become invalid in certain situations? The question then becomes "Why?" What opposing concept comes into play that defines the border of an extreme? This leading into ambiguity is the challenge to students to make meaningful distinctions.

For example, we can return to the concept of liberty and break down the analogy of baseball and place the concept into real situations. The teacher follows the questions by asking the reasons for the student's opinion. You will quickly bump into the concepts of equality and justice. Then you must pursue those concepts.

- Does the state have an obligation to provide elementary education to children?
- Should it provide middle school education?
- Should it provide high school education?
  - ▷ What if someone does not take advantage of the opportunity, but a few years later wants to pursue her education? Should this be allowed?

ઝ What if you want to attend college? Should the state provide college so that you can further achieve your potential?

    ▷   What if your state school does not have the same resources as a private school? Should the state college have the same resources as the best private colleges?

ઝ What if you want to be a doctor? Should it provide further education beyond 4 years of college? Should it put you through medical school?

ઝ What if everyone wants to be a doctor? How will you decide who deserves to go? Or should everyone be able to become a doctor?

How Many?

For the dialogue, are all of these elements necessary? How many are necessary? This will depend on the concept, the points you wish to cover, and the type of sequence you wish to teach. Form follows function. Many dialogues require only examples and counterexamples. Others will be a series of hypotheticals. Still others will have these three elements but no analogies. It is entirely up to you. The task is to clear the path for the students. Their reactions will be the evidence for whether the steps are being followed.

In general, the process is that the teacher formulates more questions, analogies, examples, counterexamples, and hypotheticals than are necessary and then steps back to review, select, and order them. You reject some, and refine and reorder the remaining ones. It is a process of expansion and contraction. You want to make the number of steps to each destination as small and effective as possible. You do not want too many steps, because then students will find it difficult to follow closely. A series of hypotheticals should be no more than three to seven in most cases. Three examples will drive most points home effectively. A single counterexample can reveal the flaw in a statement.

Again, it is best to begin small and local, that is, using the experience of the students, and then to build from there. Analogies, examples, counterexamples, and hypotheticals that are far removed from their experience are drained of personal significance and power. Socrates looked around the agora and found his material. The classroom, school, local community, sports, music, cinema, and current events offer much to the teacher. The connections become real and memorable.

Review your inductive sequence. Are the steps clearly in order? Are there too many steps? Where may there be disagreement or confusion? How will you manage this inductively?

Conclusion of the Dialogue

Many Socratic dialogues do not conclude! We saw that Socrates did not finish a dialogue by answering his own question, a habit that at times irritated others. But the student of Socrates learned a method of critical thinking that led to deeper understanding of the issue. In the classroom, problem-solving questioning will usually lead to a definitive answer. Analytical Socratic questioning, on the other hand, may not. It can clarify claims, issues, and problems and lead into a more open discussion. Particularly with complex issues, it is quite necessary to open the discussion format for further personal expression of the different facets of the issue and exploration of possible consequences.

In lessons using Socratic Method 1 or 2, solicit a summary through questions and direct the students to further investigation. The summary is a crucial element. Retrace the inductive steps, the important stops, and check for understanding. Your entire outline of questions in the Dialogue Binder will generally be one or two pages in length.

Socratic Method 2: Problem Solving

Problem solving is the most straightforward form of Socratic Method, and many teachers in fact use it without realizing its Socratic roots. Through inductive questions, the teacher guides the student to the logical solution of a problem. In *Meno*, Socrates leads a slave boy to a solution of a problem in geometry (Plato, c. 380 B.C.E./1997i).

The elaborate preparation in the Dialogue Binder is usually unnecessary. The teaching objectives are articulated with Bloom's revised taxonomy. Socratic Method 2 is anchored in Procedural Knowledge.

Planning this form of dialogue is simply knowing the steps of the process and having the ability to phrase and rephrase the questions patiently for clarification. You must vary the wording to prevent repetition and monotony. In a way, there is usually one road to the destination, and you just have to change the language of the signs to make sure the directions are communicated effectively. For example, in guiding the student to the solution of a problem in algebra, the teacher first asks how the problem can be expressed as a statement or question, what the unit will be in the solution, what information is known, what plan would be best (perhaps include a table, graph, or picture?), how to carry out the plan, and then how to check the work and solution. There are regular steps that the teacher takes the student through.

On a more demanding plane, this leads to encountering problems that do not neatly fit previous ones. Here the student must autonomously decide how to move.

Education often is learning processes of problem solving or analysis or evaluation. There is a process for analyzing sequences in cinema classes; for understanding the formal qualities of painting, sculpture, and architecture; for articulating the formal qualities of poetry; for editing a piece of writing; for the application of the scientific method; for translating a Latin sentence; and for solving math problems.

Socratic Method 2 is the facilitation of movement of problem solving into Bloom's category of application. In the application category, the student is confronted with a new problem and *without prompting* must understand this problem as well as the appropriate principles and process for its solution. In Pólya's succinct formulation, the broad steps are *Understand, Take Apart, Put Together, Check* (Pólya & Anning, 1935). The expectation is that this skill of problem solving transfers to real-life situations that are not identical to the problems encountered in the classroom. This is the entire point of Socratic Method at any level of education, whether it be elementary school or law school. The teacher facilitates the passage from *We do* to *you do.*

Usually any teacher will know the process thoroughly, and writing down the steps beforehand is unnecessary. Although there are subjects that are devoted to problem solving (e.g., mathematics), this sort of analytical dialogue again can be one phase of a larger discussion. For instance, the discussion of a love sonnet by Shakespeare will usually take into account formal properties that express and enhance more graduated meanings. A metrical analysis will not only point out iambic pentameter, but how there are conscious deviations from this, such as the insertion of trochees, to strike a word or concept more emphatically. Strategies such as alliteration or rhyming bring concepts and feelings into alignment. The teacher can call attention to the contrasting forms of the Petrarchan or Spenserian sonnet. You isolate metaphors and similes. All of these formal properties contribute to the nuanced expression of the poet's thoughts and feelings. Those thoughts and feelings then are discussed in a more open manner. Is Shakespeare in love or merely infatuated? What is the difference? Is infatuation an early phase of love that will evolve or is it just physical attraction that will quickly pass? Are there songs today that express these same feelings and ideas? Does Shakespeare's sonnet share any qualities with rap music? Could you put Shakespeare's sonnet to music today?

Uniting the Methods

The two Socratic Methods can be united in many different ways. For instance, one effective way to organize the dialogue is to borrow the structure of the argumentative essay. Select a controversial issue (e.g., Should wild animals be kept in zoos?). Through questioning, you facilitate the defining of this issue, its key terms, and its concepts. Do animals have rights? What is an animal? What is a right? Can we justify keeping an animal behind bars for our entertainment? For our education? Then, search for a position or solution by examining arguments and counterarguments. The discussion has a clear introduction, development, and conclusion (which can be open, depending on the issue). The development contrasts argument with counterargument, making an evaluation on the basis of clear principles and evidence. This form of Socratic discussion immediately transfers into learning how to write an argumentative essay, which is a key critical thinking skill in secondary education that goes beyond school.

One can adopt other essay forms to shape an inductive dialogue, linking the activity to learning the form itself of the essay. The format could be the five-paragraph essay, the cause and effect essay, the compare and contrast essay, or a literary commentary. It could be a persuasive speech. The class can even write a collective poem inductively. The form can be taken from scientific writing using the standard IMRAD formula: Introduction, Methods, Results, and Discussion. Some of these dialogues obviously may require more preparatory work. Each format has the advantage of developing further aspects of critical thinking tied to a specific subject.

The Student Preparation Sheet

Informing the students about the content and purpose of the dialogue allows them to prepare themselves. For shorter problem-solving dialogues, depending on the kind of problem, this perhaps will not be necessary. But to begin to think about and discuss a concept is a demanding task for the spur of the moment. What Socrates asked people was really quite difficult. If the concept, issue, or problem flows from the textbook or another assigned text, this should be made clear in preparatory questions. The students should know beforehand the concept, issue, or problem, the purpose of the dialogue, and usually the opening question.

Beyond these elements, you should ask the students for their ideas regarding the concept, and especially what they find difficult or confusing in understanding and applying it. This allows you to foresee problems so you are prepared to untangle the knot of confusion.

Conclusion

H. G. Wells once said, "It is not much good thinking of a thing unless you think it out." The Socratic Method teaches students how to think a concept out logically. In preparing, you must visualize the dialogue's purpose and path, but at the same time realize that a truly Socratic dialogue always adapts to the student's reactions and responses. *In authentic Socratic dialogues, the teacher's questions are suggested by the student's answers.* The teacher must listen carefully to the student's answers, perceive the student's understanding or misunderstanding, and then guide the student with questions to greater clarity, to more correct reasoning, or to further exploration. Listening is fundamentally important.

In *Gorgias*, we see an instructive example of the difficulty or futility of Socratic examination without planning or having thought through the issue. Having drawn the eminent Gorgias into an admission that one must know a subject and not simply appear persuasive, Socrates must meet the objections of a zealous young Greek supporter of Gorgias by the name of Polus. He invites Polus to either ask or answer the questions. Full of passion, Polus wants to take the initiative and so begins to ask questions, but quickly loses the way with the first response (Plato, c. 385 B.C.E./1997f). He does not know how to lead the examination. He interviews Socrates to an extent, but cannot truly examine him. He does not know the destinations or the steps to them. Socrates soon suggests questions for his own examination to the young man.

Socratic Method 1 does require meticulous planning. In the beginning, combining it with more open discussion facilitates the transition to this rigorous form of thinking. One can develop the Socratic dialogue in different ways, but keeping the inductive structure clear for the students is important, or they will feel bewildered, as Meno and others did.

In the next chapter, we will examine how to conduct a dialogue in the classroom.

Chapter 4

TAKE THE STUDENTS WITH YOU
Conducting a Socratic Dialogue

> The common reproach against me is that I am always asking questions of other people but never express my own views of anything . . .
>
> —Plato, *Theaetetus*

Conducting a Socratic dialogue in the classroom is an art that requires practice and experience. The teacher becomes the tennis pro, in the metaphor of one seasoned practitioner of Socratic questioning (Powell, 1995), who gradually challenges and leads the students forward to confront areas of difficulty. In part, the tennis pro trains her pupil verbally. Besides verbal advice, she models the behavior and movements, challenging the pupil to ascend to another level of play. Practice and experience are paramount for improvement.

For this to happen in the classroom, it is important to prepare thoroughly and to know the steps and movement of the inductive outline so that you are not chained to the desk in the front, eyes nervously scanning for the correct line of print. The routine of reviewing the night before and the morning of the dialogue traces the turns of the inductive path clearly in mind. If you know the map, you can take the students with you.

At the same time, it is important to be acutely aware of the students, because any Socratic dialogue requires a high level of engagement from them. You foster engagement by teaching students about Socrates and his method; by preparing the students for the specific dialogue; by creating a climate for participation; by selecting important and relevant issues, concepts, and problems; and especially by conducting the dialogue with patience, kindness, and clarity. An extraordinary tool for learning critical thinking, the Socratic Method can lift student thinking to another plane if conducted in a nonthreatening manner.

For all of the planning that the Socratic Method entails, the spontaneous participation of the students is an absolute necessity, or the experience becomes a very odd kind of interactive monologue. The exploration and clarification of the students' ideas through a shared investigation is the whole aim of any authentic dialogue. If you do not take the students along, there is no point in making the journey.

Preparation Sheet for Students

Providing a preparation sheet with the concept, the reading or viewing assignment, and preliminary questions facilitates participation. The preparation sheet (see p.140) should be given a week before the dialogue. The students then should know the assignment, the objectives as well as the central claim, concept, issue, and problem. They know the type of Socratic dialogue—problem solving or analytical. With these fundamental elements understood, the experience becomes more familiar and more meaningful.

To facilitate further, you can assign key ideas, issues, or questions to specific students. In this way, the students have a more focused preparation and can become experts on one facet of the discussion. This also allows you to diversify the Socratic discussion from the very beginning.

A Safe Environment

Creating a safe environment is fundamentally important. Each student will have her or his own perspective on ideas, issues, and problems. Each will have different reactions and responses to the questions. You most often find that students (and really pretty much all of us!) regard the basis for their opinions and attitudes as self-evident. To examine the basis, comparing it with alternative points of view, is challenging and pulls someone from his or her comfort zone. For authentic engagement and participation, you need to foster a rapport of trust.

The goal of Socratic questioning is not to learn a few points about a text, but to think critically about a concept, issue, or problem, patiently considering other points of view. The student is not to learn an official interpretation to be repeated on a test. The student must think for herself or himself. In the Socratic classroom, the students must know that their feelings, opinions, beliefs, and knowledge are valuable and important for the discussion. They should feel comfortable. Conducting a Socratic discussion requires social and emotional intelligence, not just critical thinking.

At the same time, you must not collapse the dialogue into a simple relativism (everyone is right), for this circumvents genuine critical thought. In examining the bases and consequences of different points of view, challenge the students to think more seriously about concepts, issues, and problems.

Listen Carefully

Socratic questioning, while planned, is completely open to the responses of the other person. Follow-up questions are in response to answers. So it is extremely important to listen to and understand the responses, not to hurry inattentively to the next question on the outline. The student may suggest the next question. The pace should be walking or jogging, not running and sprinting. If you run, you can't listen.

One should also listen without reacting dramatically, without a dry laugh, or raising the voice, or hitting a word with a new pitch, or hurrying the pace (one of the signs of debate). Listen without appearing to judge.

Listen reflectively. Rephrase an unclear response and ask, "Is this what you mean? Is this what you feel?" A variation would be to ask another student to rephrase the response. You can repeat key words in the paraphrasing. Make empathetic comments.

Observe. Nonverbal communication tells us a great deal—whether we can probe further, whether we should be more restrained. The comfort level of the student will be manifested physically as well as in the tone of voice, the pace of speech, and the words used. Socratic questioning should not be inquisitional. Observe the reactions of the students.

Socratic Irony: Be Nice, But Do Not Give the Answer!

Much ink has been spilled about the irony of Socrates, and his use of irony does have different facets and nuances. Socrates claimed not to know the answers to the big questions he posed. At times, his listeners felt he knew more and was not being candid; at other times, they felt mocked, which would always be out of place in the classroom.

But there are many grains of wisdom in the refusal to give answers. Giving answers stops student thinking. The student often believes the answer is certain and beyond criticism (or at least will get them past the quiz or test!), and mental effort halts.

Not answering the question with a declarative paragraph shifts the burden of understanding gently onto the shoulders of the student, who must work out the concept or issue step by step. Nothing is prepackaged and simply memorized for future paraphrasing on a quiz or test.

In general, it is a preferable never to give answers. Redirect questions. Ask students to clarify, to offer information. This is not thoughtless following of Socratic practice, because the objective is to stimulate critical thought.

Follow-Up Questions

Follow up questions (see Figure 5) are vitally important. They maintain the flow of discussion and allow the teacher to ascertain how well the student understands. These questions are in response to the answer by the student.

Learning the Basic Terms of Arguments

Teaching the students the basic vocabulary of critical thinking opens many windows. This will be further elaborated in the next chapter. Too many terms will confuse the students, but a few provide compass points for orientation. The selection may vary according to subject, but I suggest beginning with the six terms in Figure 6.

Clarify	Challenge	Consequences	Connect
What do you mean by that?	What evidence is there for that?	What will happen if . . . ? (hypothetical)	How can you connect this to the text?
Can you clarify this word?	Is there another point of view?		Can you link this with what X said?
What do you think about this?	Can you think of an example?		
Can you say this in another way?	Is there a counterexample?		

Figure 5. Follow-up questions.

Claim	A statement that is either true or false.
Premise	A statement (claim) that is a reason for believing the conclusion.
Conclusion	A statement that is supported by the premise(s). The conclusion can become a premise in a continuing chain of reasoning.
Argument	Often this word is used as a synonym for quarrel, but in the academic context it more often means a series of reasons to support a claim that is called the conclusion. In an argument someone gives reasons for believing *that something is true*. The conclusion of an argument can become a premise in another argument.
Value Judgment	A statement of the goodness or merit of something. The criteria for judgment should be clearly defined and understood.
Explanation	An explanation gives reasons *why something is as it is*. The something is already accepted as true. An explanation is different from an argument. In an argument, someone gives reasons for believing *that something is true*.

Figure 6. Terms of arguments.

Again, like the good tennis pro who models the skills, using the words in dialogue and discussion is important. Students become familiar with them. You can spend an entire lesson on learning these words, which are applicable in daily life. More precise thinking requires a more precise vocabulary. Other terms in argument can be learned through the year.

Wait Time

In Plato's dialogues, you do not always see Socrates pausing and waiting for the other person to think. But he must have. When asking challenging questions, you must wait for the other person to reflect and formulate a response. Hilda Taba rightly said that a fast discussion is seldom a thoughtful discussion (Durkin, 1993).

The temptation may be to jump to another student for a quick response. Wait for 5 seconds. You will have to exercise judgment, perhaps saying, "We can come back in a minute." Or perhaps you must clarify your question or ask another question entirely.

Waiting is important. Do not be intimidated by silence. How you handle it will tell the students much about education. And of course, you should not answer your own question!

Involve the Entire Class

Students should be doing most of the speaking. They should not feel grilled, as if the classroom were a courtroom. Get as many students involved as you can. If you have assigned questions to students, continue to involve them after their phase. Ask them for links and summaries. Solicit everything from the students. You can even assign them roles in the discussion, as in Figure 7.

Avoid giving explanations or minilectures. We feel at times an oracular impulse to explain. A student makes a comment or offers an insight, and we treat it as a topic sentence for a paragraph of our own clarification and elaboration. We bring in new facts, make connections, draw conclusions. In effect, the teacher has had a learning moment. Teachers do have learning moments, but we need to bring the students forward.

Can students ask questions? By all means! Student questions are signposts to new directions. Moreover, if students can assemble an inductive sequence of probing questions, this is an unmistakable sign that they are assimilating the Socratic Method. Train the students to question, not to answer.

For variety, assign and rotate roles to students for the discussion:
- Defining the concept
- Answering the first question
- Examples
- Counterexamples
- Summarizing
- Linking
- Concluding

Figure 7. Student roles.

Use the Board

One way to keep the class focused on the central question is to put it on the screen or whiteboard. Does everyone understand the question? Students can rephrase it in their own words. Then begin the exploration of answers.

Write down the major points made by the students. This affirms their value and allows for clarity and focused exploration.

To some extent, one can plan the board and visualize what may be written down. Make the board interesting, with arrows, simple figures, and dialogue clouds. Pictures, graphs, and tables can also contribute to evidence.

Signposts and Summaries

Signpost questions are very important. These questions indicate the direction of the inquiry. "What is the claim? What conclusion must we draw?" These allow the student to better understand the structure of the dialogue.

At the end of each phase, there should be a summary. Solicit the summary from students. As the dialogue extends, the summary should also link to previous phases. You should be continually checking for understanding and clarifying what is necessary.

"Can you summarize what has been said?" is a question that requires the students to gather the ideas expressed by other students, and, in doing this, to help other students comprehend what has happened in the discussion. To summarize every 10 minutes is helpful. You can also appoint summarizers whose job is to report back to the group on what has been said.

Be Funny

Socrates was a funny man. He looked funny, knew how to take a joke, and knew how to make jokes. His humor is revealed in different ways in the dialogues—at times gentle, at other times more blunt. Humor relieves tension, relaxes the group, and can light a different angle to a subject. At its best, humor gives insight.

But humor can be tricky. Questions and humor can unintentionally mix to make a student feel mocked, which is never desirable, so be sure the humor is directed at yourself or some aspect of the topic or situation, never the student's answer. Have humorous examples and counterexamples—they are the bedrock for standup comedians commenting on weird or absurdly difficult aspects of daily life.

But do be careful when making the quip. Think before you leap into humor.

Reflect on the Experience

Oscar Wilde famously said that experience is the name everyone gives to their mistakes. Keep track of your experiences in the Dialogue Binder. Look at the objectives of the class, and honestly assess whether they were attained. Have the students made progress in their understanding of the claim, concept, issue, or problem? Have the students made progress in understanding how to think critically? Make notes about the comments and participation of individual students. Discuss the experience with a colleague.

One of the best methods of professional development is recording the class dialogues. By unobtrusively placing the camera in a corner of the classroom, and notifying the students that you are recording to assess your own teaching, you set the class at ease and give yourself a faithful record of the dialogue. You have the opportunity for instant replay. You can see where you fumbled and what happened when the ball was rolling around on the ground. You can observe what went well, where the chain of reasoning snapped. Were there any fouls? Would a keen referee have blown the whistle on the teacher at some point? How did the class respond to the questioning? How did you respond to the class?

Did Socrates improve his technique of questioning through reflective and repeated practice? We do not see this exactly in the dialogues, although there are dialogues when he is younger and sitting at the feet of more advanced philosophers (e.g., *Parmenides*). But no one arrives at such expert performance without practice, clarifying ideas to the point where one can intuitively locate the fundamental claim that must be examined, and then investigate this claim systematically. Practice writing questions in inductive format in short sequences to get to important destinations. Practice in class.

Keep Practicing and Be Unrelentingly Positive

The discussions in Plato's dialogues have a jewel-like literary perfection—witty, the right question at the right time, the right analogy, the right hypothetical, an insistent inductive movement ahead to conclusions. In the classroom, Socratic discussions will have more pauses, more rephrasings, more clarifications. All of this is fine.

What makes the teaching experience continuously fascinating and challenging is that every class, every single student, is different. Keeping the dialogues relatively short and clearly signposted makes them more helpful to the students. After finishing, review the inductive steps to the conclusion or generalization. The learning of the students is on two rails: the first is the investigation of the selected claim, concept, issue, or problem; the second is the process itself of critical thinking. In terms of Bloom's revised taxonomy, the first rail is the knowledge dimension, the second the cognitive dimension.

Learning to think like Socrates requires repeated short, appropriately challenging experiences, not punishing and exhausting marathons. Short dialogues of 5–7 minutes allow the students to become familiar with the concepts in more open discussion. It is the jog and walk method. Jog for a few minutes, then walk for recovery. As the semester goes on, you can increase the minutes of jogging (not racing) in Socratic dialogue. You never want to phase out the walking in open discussion. More open discussion is always important, but it also will become more rigorously structured as students learn the expectations of critical thinking. They see the extent of belief, the borders of knowledge, the possibilities of truth.

Socratic teaching also draws the students away from facile relativism or the idea that everyone is right. Tolerance is an important virtue in a multi-cultural society, and obviously there are many perspectives on important issues in the world. But this does not mean that one must refrain from examination of these other points of view, investigating their assumptions and consequences. Everyone has a right to a point of view, but not all points of view are equally correct.

Ten Commandments of Socratic Questioning

Irving Younger, a famous teacher of legal cross examination, developed 10 commandments for lawyers to keep in mind in the examination of witnesses. Teachers are not cross examiners (teaching is much harder), but the idea of providing guidelines or commandments is appealing given the misconceptions that have developed in the past concerning the application of the Socratic Method. There have been times, if you read some of the worst experiences of law students, when it was considered a contact sport, the teacher chasing a zig-zagging student down the field of discussion.

These are my 10 Commandments for Socratic Questioning.

1. You shall not question without understanding the concept or issue.
2. You shall never humiliate a student.
3. You shall be friendly and unrelentingly positive.
4. You shall ask simple and clear questions in inductive sequences.
5. You shall not lecture with questions.
6. You shall listen carefully to answers.
7. You shall check for personal understanding.
8. You shall ask students to summarize.
9. You shall teach the students to question inductively.
10. You shall reflect on your teaching regularly.

Chapter 5

CULTIVATING GADFLIES
Teaching Students the Socratic Method

> I think we can be pretty sure someone understands something when he can make someone else understand it.
> —Plato, *Alcibiades*

Before beginning a Socratic dialogue, it is extraordinarily helpful to teach the students about Socrates and his method. Knowing the life of the great philosopher and how he taught people in ancient Athens frames the experience of the classroom dialogue and reveals to students how questioning can be used in education. They understand how the most basic aim of a Socratic dialogue is either the examination of a claim or the solution of a problem. Students become more conscious of how thought can develop through inductive questioning.

Not only is it important to teach *about* the Socratic Method, it is important to teach the students the method, that is, teach the students how to plan and conduct a Socratic dialogue, not how to undergo one. In conducting short discussions, they learn how to question inductively, how challenging this is, and what mistakes can be made. Through this they learn how to participate actively in Socratic dialogue. Postman and Weingartner (1969) put it bluntly: "Asking questions is behavior. If you don't do it, you don't learn it" (p. 24).

At a minimum, this introduction to the Socratic Method entails devoting three class periods to reading closely and discussing short excerpts from the works of Plato and Xenophon. (See the lesson plans on p. 80.) The selections introduce students to the basic elements and dynamics of the Socratic

Method in a graduated manner. In discussing the passages with students, I make clear that as interesting and relevant as the philosophical ideas of Plato often are, we are focusing on the inductive method of questioning. How does Socrates guide the other person?

The learning then moves to writing a short dialogue, and then planning an interactive dialogue. It is possible to teach middle school and high school students the basics of Socratic questioning. Through further lessons in analogies and hypotheticals, students can develop skills in critical examination.

These are the lessons:

1.   What is induction, and how can questions lead to a conclusion?
2.   How can we analyze through questions?
3.   What are slippery slopes and order bias?

Class 1: What Is Induction, and How Can Questions Lead to a Conclusion?

Before looking at the Socratic passages, beginning with a selection from *Lysis* (Plato, c. 390 B.C.E./1997h, 207d–210c), I teach the students the fundamentals of inductive reasoning. Induction leads to a discovery (see Figure 8), and in Plato's early Socratic dialogues, this discovery was often the painful realization of a lack of knowledge. But in a contemporary classroom, the discovery clearly can be anything. Inductive reasoning, still much debated by philosophers, is an integral part of the science curriculum and can be easily recognized in daily life (Mak, Mak, & Mak, 2009).

Induction usually works in one of two ways. First, you can reason from past events to a generalization about the present and future. In this way, we use induction every day. When we go grocery shopping, we may notice that products in the small store in the neighborhood cost more than those in the large supermarket in the mall. Then we notice that on the Internet, they may cost even less than in the supermarket. From these instances, we infer that the cost of overhead drops with large stores and plummets with the Internet. This means that products can be purchased cheaply in large supermarkets, and even more cheaply online. Our experience of selected past events allows us to generalize about the present and future.

Secondly, using a formulation that is not necessarily past–future related, we can reason inductively from selected observations to a generalization. Many believe inductive reasoning to be integral to the scientific method,

Induction leads to a discovery.

Induction usually works in one of two ways:

1. From past events to a generalization about the present and future

2. From selected observations to a generalization

Induction is never certain, but is probable. An inductive argument can be weak (less probable) or strong (more probable)

Figure 8. Induction.

and so responsible for the extraordinary strides in science and technology that have transformed the world during the last 400 years. Science proceeds through myriad activities, including observation, measurement, the formulation of hypotheses, experimentation, and the recording of data. The reasoner seeks patterns and explanations (i.e., theories and models) for natural phenomena that are accurate in prediction. Through induction, you arrive at and criticize scientific facts, hypotheses, theories, and laws. Science is constantly open to revision. It is self-correcting.

In middle school and high school, students will be familiar with this basic application of inductive reasoning in science. In the Socratic Method, the class is ideally moving in the same inductive manner to greater clarity in understanding.

The Problem With Induction: Not Certain

Induction does have a problem, in that it does not offer certainty. Looking at a collection of instances is helpful, but any generalization in the collection can be subverted by a single contradictory case. Within the sphere of science, perhaps the most often repeated example of this is the case of swans. For centuries it was believed that all swans were white. The strong inductive line of reasoning was, *Every swan ever observed has been white, therefore, all swans are white.* But the discovery of the black swan in Australia in the 18th century undermined this generalization.

To return to a previous example, although in general it may be cheaper to buy over the Internet, the small store down the street may have a sale next week, and something we desire to buy may cost less there than in the supermarket or online. Our experience is open to reevaluation. Similarly, our understanding of conclusions and generalizations often is open to modification with further consideration of more cases.

Teaching Induction: Reverse the Outline

With the basic understanding of induction established, you can teach the students how to think inductively in a more conscious manner. They now learn to lead another person to a conclusion through a series of points. As Sherlock Holmes told an astonished Dr. Watson in "The Adventure of the Dancing Men," "You see, my dear Watson . . . it is not really difficult to construct a series of inferences, each dependent upon its predecessor and each simple in itself" (Doyle, 1905, p. 62). As always, Holmes was right.

Most students learn how to outline in elementary and middle school. One effective way of teaching induction, and how to lead another person inductively to a conclusion, is to reverse the outline format that students have learned. In conventional outlining, students create a heading and then list the supporting details under the heading (see Figure 9).

Now, put this into question form, elaborating with more lively details of dialogue, and you are on the way to writing a Socratic dialogue.

Backward planning is essential. One begins with the conclusion.

How Can Inductive Questions Lead to a Conclusion? A Passage From Plato's Lysis

Explaining induction can be done quickly, and it is up to the teacher whether the explanation will come before or after the reading and discussion of the passage from Plato's *Lysis* (c. 390 B.C.E./1997h, 207d–210c). If you proceed inductively, first read the passage from Plato, and allow the students to discover the guiding principles of the questioning on their own, leading them with questions as necessary. On the other hand, if you explain induction before the discussion of the texts, then the students have been alerted and recognize the principles without work.

Next, through a brief selection from Plato's *Lysis*, students examine the inductive use of examples or analogies as steps to a conclusion. *Lysis* focuses on the question "What is friendship?" Socrates has just left the Academy and is on the way to the Lyceum when an acquaintance greets him and ushers him into a wrestling school, where the two meet a group of friends. There is banter about love and friendship, and Socrates soon engages the young Lysis in a conversation. Socrates demonstrates that Lysis is not as free as he believed, and that the lack of knowledge and understanding are the reasons for his lack of freedom.

Although the dialogue extends into an examination of friendship, an examination very much rooted in the Athenian culture of antiquity, my focus

---

Conventional Outline:

Between 1400 and 1600 sculpture often imitated classical works of art.

Sculptures were often made in marble or bronze.

The figures were sometimes nude.

The figures often stood in *contrapposto*.

Their proportions were based on Greek and Roman statues.

An inductive argument outline works in the opposite direction. One first lists the supporting details, then the generalization or conclusion:

Sculptures between 1400 and 1600 were often made in marble or bronze.

Their figures were sometimes nude.

Their figures often stood in *contrapposto*.

Their proportions were based on Greek and Roman statues.

Figure 9. Conventional outline and inductive outline.

---

in teaching the passage is on the manner of questioning at the beginning of the work. Socrates asks questions that move from example to example, each drawn from the experience of Lysis, that collectively drive to a conclusion. Without prodding, students clearly see that Socrates knows where to lead the conversation, and that he has selected his conclusion and examples carefully. If he were doing this spontaneously, he would have already thought about the question beforehand.

Students should be clear on four points:

1. Socrates knows his conclusion first.
2. He selects examples to lead to the conclusion.
3. He uses short questions with one statement, seeking agreement.
4. Lysis arrives at a discovery.

The extension activity for this class is writing a single-page inductive dialogue. This can be on any topic, or you can suggest an idea such as equality, which has many facets to be explored. This assignment can be challenging for students, but the challenge is healthy, because it familiarizes them with inductive reasoning. Emphasize the importance of making an outline before writing. Jumping into the writing of questions without a clear destination will be baffling and frustrating. Students should establish the conclusion first, then visualize the steps necessary to reach the conclusion. They can elaborate further by expanding points into subpoints.

INTERVIEW	SOCRATIC QUESTIONING
Questions and answers	Questions and answers
Facts and opinions	Facts and opinions
Not usually driving to a conclusion	Pointed to a conclusion
Not usually focused on analysis and evaluation	Always focused on analysis and evaluation
Not inductive	Inductive reasoning
	Usually seeks assent to series of statements

Figure 10. The differences between an interview and Socratic questioning.

It is important for students to visualize clearly the person with whom they are conversing. Equality, surprisingly, can be a divisive issue, and the identity of the interlocutor will partially determine the questions.

Read and discuss the dialogues in class. Ask students to articulate their difficulties. One common mistake is to write an interview rather than an inductive dialogue. An interview solicits information, and often there is not a systematic examination of assumptions and consequences. To make clear the difference between an interview and Socratic questioning, I write a table, as shown in Figure 10, on the board.

Class 2: How Can We Analyze Through Questions? A Passage From Xenophon's Memorabilia.

Next, through the reading and analysis of a selection from Xenophon's (c. 371 B.C.E./1994) *Memorabilia* (see Book 4, Chapter 2, pp. 1–24), students learn how to analyze through inductive questions, suggesting hypothetical situations or counterexamples.

In this passage, Xenophon wishes to demonstrate how Socrates varied his approach to questioning according to the person before him. In this imagined story, Socrates encounters Euthydemus, a young man who has gathered a large library for learning but has not studied with a teacher. Socrates playfully chides and mocks Euthydemus, and succeeds in bringing

Unjust	Just
I. (Memoirs IV.ii.14) • Lying • Deceit • Mischief • Selling into slavery	**II. (Memoirs IV.ii.15)** • Enslaving an unjust city • Deceiving the enemy • Plundering the enemy **III. (Memoirs IV.ii.16-17)** • Lying and deceit of a general to prevent discouragement of the troops • Lying and deceit of a father to have child take medicine • Taking and hiding the sword from a person not in his right mind

Figure 11. Just and unjust.

him into a conversation about justice, whose principles he must understand in order to take the leading role in Athenian life he wishes.

To clarify their ideas, Socrates makes use of a graphic organizer: he draws a table for Unjust and Just, as in Figure 11, and Euthydemus then must choose to which different actions should be assigned. He quickly puts lying, deceit, mischief, and selling into slavery into the Unjust category. Then Socrates suggests a series of hypothetical situations with these actions, and the young man realizes he must put them all under the Just heading. Although the examples are very much rooted in Athenian society, where slavery was accepted, and especially in the military experience of the author, contemporary students enjoy this passage more than the selection from *Lysis*.

Euthydemus is driven to the conclusion that he needs to learn more about justice and injustice, and that learning with a teacher is better than solitary study with books. He discovers his own ignorance. If Socrates had said at the beginning that Euthydemus did not understand justice and injustice, and that learning with an experienced teacher is better than solitary study, and had delivered a lecture on these two points, would Euthydemus have accepted his claims?

What is different in this selection from Xenophon is that the reader explores other lines of thought with examples, and must compare and contrast these lines and their conclusions. The dialogue pivots in a new direction with a statement by Euthydemus ("I thought we were talking about relationships with enemies"), and the analysis pursues a different direction.

To extend the learning, I assign the writing of a one-page dialogue on an aspect of equality. For this, we look at four aspects of equality:

- ❧ Physical and intellectual equality
- ❧ Equality in human dignity
- ❧ Socioeconomic equality
- ❧ Equality in opportunity

The development of the aspects can be done in this way. First, it is necessary to define equality, so that all of the students are thinking about the same idea. After this, one can assign a different aspect of equality to individuals for development in an inductive outline with examples and counterexamples.

In examining equality, students will find that they must learn something about justice and fairness as well. This requires finding a resource that succinctly clarifies issues within justice, and how these impact questions of equality. The Internet will provide several such resources that are accessible to students.

Having brainstormed the aspects of equality, now the students can prepare the inductive outlines learned in the previous lesson. With the skeleton of ideas, they can then compose a dramatic Socratic dialogue. Read the dialogues in class.

Class 3: Slippery Slopes and Order Bias

Sequence is all in the Socratic Method. Individual questions are important, but the inductive sequence is a distinguishing characteristic, and errors in sequencing can be made. In attempting to use the Socratic Method, students will understand that the chain of reasoning is not always correct; the questioner may make a confusing misstep, asking the other person to accept a point that does not necessarily follow. A valid objection can be made to the chain of reasoning. The purpose of the third lesson is to review two common mistakes of this kind. The issue is not that a single link in the chain is defective, but that the entire chain has flaws and its principle of organization is fallacious.

Slippery Slope

The slippery slope is a fallacy in which a weak sequence of causes leads to a negative or undesired conclusion. If we allow A, then B will follow; if

B, then C; if C, then D. If we do not want D, we cannot permit A. The negative consequence is crucial, causing a jump to an unwarranted conclusion, namely that A should not be allowed.

At first, the sequence looks like a hypothetical syllogism, a valid chain of reasoning. What makes the chain of reasoning fallacious is the degree of likelihood that B must follow. In the fallacy, B seems to follow, whereas in reality the step to B is not inevitable or necessary or likely. Allegations of the slippery slope fallacy occur in political debates about gun control, same-sex marriage, or any other measure restricting liberty. Whether the measure concerns a controversial or politically charged issue, the idea is that taking the first step leads inexorably to the second and so on to the last. The first step is regarded as the "thin edge of the wedge."

Order Bias

Professional pollsters and other writers of questionnaires have long cautioned against sequencing questions in a manipulative way that guides the respondent to a desired emotional response. Called order bias, this sequence pushes the respondent ahead by emotional responses, not justified reasons. Some years ago this was humorously captured in a British sitcom called *Yes, Prime Minister*. In this episode, the prime minister sees that a survey indicates that the public wishes to reestablish the draft (called National Service), and so he will push ahead with this mission. But the wily senior civil servant, Sir Humphrey, shocked at the minister's poor judgment and wishing to prevent the reintroduction of the draft, decides to conduct another survey that will reveal that the people in reality do not want it. Sir Humphrey maintains and demonstrates that, through questions, manipulative polls can arrive at any desired conclusion.

> **Humphrey:** You know what happens: Nice young lady comes up to you. Obviously you want to create a good impression, you don't want to look a fool, do you? So she starts asking you some questions: "Mr. Woolley, are you worried about the number of young people without jobs?"
>
> **Bernard:** Yes.
>
> **Humphrey:** "Are you worried about the rise in crime among teenagers?"
>
> **Bernard:** Yes.
>
> **Humphrey:** "Do you think there is a lack of discipline in our Comprehensive schools?"
>
> **Bernard:** Yes.

Humphrey: "Do you think young people welcome some authority and leadership in their lives?"

Bernard: Yes.

Humphrey: "Do you think they respond to a challenge?"

Bernard: Yes.

Humphrey: "Would you be in favor of reintroducing National Service?"

Bernard: Oh . . . well, I suppose I might be.

Humphrey: "Yes or no?"

Bernard: Yes.

Humphrey: Of course you would, Bernard. After all you told her you can't say no to that. So they don't mention the first five questions and they publish the last one.

Bernard: Is that really what they do?

Humphrey: Well, not the reputable ones, no, but there aren't many of those. So alternatively the young lady can get the opposite result.

Bernard: How?

Humphrey: "Mr. Woolley, are you worried about the danger of war?"

Bernard: Yes.

Humphrey: "Are you worried about the growth of armaments?"

Bernard: Yes.

Humphrey: "Do you think there is a danger in giving young people guns and teaching them how to kill?"

Bernard: Yes.

Humphrey: "Do you think it is wrong to force people to take up arms against their will?"

Bernard: Yes.

Humphrey: "Would you oppose the reintroduction of National Service?"

Bernard: Yes.

Humphrey: There you are, you see Bernard. The perfect balanced sample. (Jay, Lynn, & Lotterby, 1986)

Entertaining as the satirical exchange is, obviously this is not a proper survey, because it is manipulative and only seeks to provoke a desired response. It is not Socratic questioning, for the questions do not inductively clarify and analyze ideas, challenge assertions and assumptions, examine any alternative points of view, or predict consequences. They do not extend thought critically and meaningfully. They do not inductively lead the other person to an important discovery.

But the exchange is instructive, for it demonstrates how leading questioning can be manipulative, emotionally forcing a conclusion without a proper argument. Order bias is a form of seduction.

Conclusion

Many dialogues by Plato are easier to read than plays by Shakespeare. In middle school and the first 2 years of high school, it is not uncommon for students to read *Julius Caesar, Romeo and Juliet,* or *Macbeth.* Shakespeare's vocabulary and literary conventions are difficult for many students, and yet they struggle through to achieve benefits. Students are also capable of reading some of the most important works of Plato.

In reading the passages from Plato and Xenophon, students quickly recognize how smart the figure of Socrates is. They will also be able to articulate that he must know the conclusion from the very beginning. He knows exactly where he wants the discussion to go, and the direction is clear and unswerving. Moreover, the students will also understand that the examples must be selected after reflection on the conclusion.

If you pursue passages from other dialogues, or some of the shorter dialogues, students realize that Socrates not only mastered a method, but that Plato had amazing ideas that are still relevant today. The story of the Ring of Gyges or the dilemma of Euthyphro provoke discussion. This is not to exalt the classics over contemporary works, staging another Swiftian Battle of the Books, for the students should read many things, from Plato to Vernor Vinge. But after reading Plato, they will better appreciate Vernor Vinge.

It is important to start with simplicity, so that students can confidently establish procedural knowledge, that is, how they can construct an inductive argument. From here they can learn to examine conflicting claims. You can also expand these lessons into greater complexity in other ways. For instance, you can examine analogies, exploring what makes a strong or weak analogy, how they can be used in dialogues. For analogies, you can select a passage from Mark Twain's (1917) Socratic dialogue, *What Is Man?,* a work written in a more pessimistic time of his life. Students can also assemble a series of hypothetical situations to test a concept. Through cultivating these skills, they become true partners in the Socratic exploration.

Three Lesson Plans: Introducing the Socratic Method

Induction and the Use of Examples: Lysis

OVERVIEW

Students will closely read and discuss a passage from Plato's *Lysis*. This brief passage is not to be read for the ideas of Socrates on friendship, but only for the method used in questioning.

OBJECTIVES

The students will:

- *understand* induction,
- *examine* and understand the use of examples, and
- *read* and understand a passage from Plato's dialogue *Lysis*.

COMMON CORE STATE STANDARDS

English Language Arts Standards: Reading: Informational Text

Standard 2: Determine a central idea of a text and analyze its development over the course of the text, including its relationship to supporting ideas; provide an objective summary of the text.

Standard 8: Delineate and evaluate the argument and specific claims in a text, assessing whether the reasoning is sound and the evidence is relevant and sufficient; recognize when irrelevant evidence is introduced.

English Language Arts Standards: Speaking & Listening

Comprehension and Collaboration:

Standard 1a: Come to discussions prepared, having read or researched material under study; explicitly draw on that preparation by referring to evidence on the topic, text, or issue to probe and reflect on ideas under discussion

Standard 3: Delineate a speaker's argument and specific claims, evaluating the soundness of the reasoning and relevance and sufficiency of the evidence and identifying when irrelevant evidence is introduced.

RESOURCES/MATERIALS

Copies of *Lysis* 207d–210c (ending with Lysis saying "I agree"). Passages may be taken from Jowett's Victorian translation available in several places on the Internet (e.g., http://www.gutenberg.org; http://www.archive.org; http://classics.mit.edu).

PROCEDURE

1. Induction
   - ▶ If the students are unsure of the method of induction, use the board to write collectively a conclusion and a series of steps.
2. Background
   - ▶ Plato's *Lysis* focuses on the question, "What is friendship?" Socrates has just left the Academy and is on his way to the Lyceum, when an acquaintance greets him and ushers him into a wrestling school, where the two meet a group of friends. There is banter about love and friendship, and Socrates engages the young Lysis in a conversation.
   - ▶ In assigning the extension activity, stress the need to make an inductive outline, not to try to write without knowing where the dialogue is going. Remind the students that the dialogue needs inductive movement.
3. Questions
   - ▶ Opening:
     - i. What is happening in this passage?
     - ii. What do you think of Socrates? What makes you say this?
     - iii. What is Socrates trying to do?
   - ▶ Close Reading
     - i. How does Socrates guide the young man to a conclusion?
     - ii. List the examples used by Socrates.
     - iii. Do you notice any direction in the arrangement of the examples?
     - iv. How many facts does Socrates include in a question?
     - v. Why does he use just one fact? Why not two or three?
     - vi. What is inductive reasoning?
     - vii. How does Sherlock Holmes solve his crimes?
     - viii. How is Socrates inductively guiding Lysis?
     - ix. Has Socrates helped Lysis learn something?
     - x. What conclusion does Lysis reach at the end of the passage?
   - ▶ Exploratory
     - i. Do you agree with the conclusion?
     - ii. Do you use inductive reasoning in daily life? How?
   - ▶ Concluding
     - i. Have you seen this type of questioning in school? Have teachers tried to guide you by questions? Is it helpful or confusing? How?
     - ii. Is dialogue a good method for learning or do you prefer other methods? What place should it have in the classroom?

EXTENSION ACTIVITIES

1. Write an updated version of the passage. Is a contemporary teenager free?
2. Write a one-page dialogue with a series of examples that guides someone inductively to a conclusion about friendship.

Lesson 2

The Use of Counterexamples: Xenophon's Memorabilia

OVERVIEW

In this lesson, students progress in their understanding of how examples and counter-examples can guide the formation of concepts. They will read a brief and vivid passage from Xenophon that shows Socrates inductively guiding a young man to a better understanding of himself and the need for a teacher. In this passage, students can observe a development of the Socratic Method, and they can also discuss the concept of justice.

OBJECTIVES

The students will:

- ✺ read and understand a passage from Xenophon,
- ✺ examine the inductive use of examples and counterexamples,
- ✺ refine their understanding of induction, and
- ✺ understand how Socrates led someone to discover ignorance.

COMMON CORE STATE STANDARDS

English Language Arts Standards: Reading: Informational Text

Standard 2: Determine a central idea of a text and analyze its development over the course of the text, including its relationship to supporting ideas; provide an objective summary of the text.

Standard 8: Delineate and evaluate the argument and specific claims in a text, assessing whether the reasoning is sound and the evidence is relevant and sufficient; recognize when irrelevant evidence is introduced.

English Language Arts Standards: Speaking & Listening
Comprehension and Collaboration:

Standard 1a: Come to discussions prepared, having read or researched material under study; explicitly draw on that preparation by referring to evidence on the topic, text, or issue to probe and reflect on ideas under discussion.

Standard 3: Delineate a speaker's argument and specific claims, evaluating the soundness of the reasoning and relevance and sufficiency of the evidence and identifying when irrelevant evidence is introduced.

RESOURCES/MATERIALS

Copies of Xenophon's *Memorabilia*, Book 4, Chapter 2, pages 1–24. Passages may be taken from H. G. Dakyns' Victorian translation available in several places on the Internet (e.g., http://www.gutenberg.org; http://www.archive.org). One can also use E. C. Marchant's translation in the Loeb series (http://www.perseus.tufts.edu). A contemporary translation by Bonnette can also be used, but it is not on the Internet.

PROCEDURE

1. Background
   - ▶ Socrates meets a young Athenian by the name of Euthydemus who believes he has learned much from books alone. Socrates will show him that reading and solitary study have not educated him sufficiently.
   - ▶ Xenophon is a colorful writer. He was a soldier and a friend of Socrates, but was away on a mercenary expedition when Socrates was arrested, tried, and sentenced to death. The military expedition, retold in a book called *Anabasis*, is a fascinating adventure story. He wrote many dialogues about Socrates, and people like Thomas Jefferson and Benjamin Franklin preferred the portrayal by Xenophon to that of Plato.
   - ▶ In assigning the extension activity, again stress the need to make an inductive outline, not to try to write without knowing where the dialogue is going. Remind the students that the dialogue needs inductive movement.
   - ▶ For further ideas on equality, consult "Dimensions of Equality" (Adler, 1984).
   - ▶ For further ideas on justice, consult Andre and Velasquez (1990).
2. Questions
   - ▶ Opening
     - i. What is happening in this passage?
     - ii. What do you think of Socrates? What makes you say this?
     - iii. What is Socrates trying to do?
   - ▶ Close Reading
     - i. How is this passage different from the passage from *Lysis*?
     - ii. How is the young man Euthydemus different from the young man Lysis?
     - iii. Write out the table made by Socrates using Justice and Injustice as headings.
     - iv. How does Socrates use examples differently from *Lysis*?
     - v. How does Socrates clarify the question without giving an answer?
     - vi. What is a closed question? (Tell them or lead inductively, with examples, to this.)
     - vii. What is an open question? (Tell them or lead inductively, with examples, to this.)
     - viii. Why doesn't Socrates give the answer? Why does he not just bluntly tell Euthydemus what he thinks?
     - ix. What conclusion does Euthydemus draw from the questioning by Socrates?
     - x. How is Euthydemus different at the end of the passage?
   - ▶ Exploratory
     - i. Do you think it is better to just be told something, or to work it out?
     - ii. Was it important for Euthydemus to discover his own ignorance?
     - iii. Is this necessary for everyone? Do we all need to do this?
     - iv. Do you agree with what Socrates demonstrates about Justice and Injustice? How would you contest him?

► Concluding
  i. Max Beerbohm, a witty English writer, once said that "The Socratic manner is not a game at which two can play." What does he mean by this? Do you agree? Why?

EXTENSION ACTIVITIES

1. Make an inductive outline and write a one-page Socratic dialogue arriving at a discovery about equality. Define equality. Choose your speakers well. They need not be anonymous people. Choose one of these aspects:
   a. physical and intellectual equality
   b. equality in human dignity
   c. socioeconomic equality
   d. equality in opportunity

2. Make an inductive outline and write a dialogue that examines contrasting points of view on a controversial issue of your choice.

3. In a group of 3–4 people, write and perform a skit of a television talk show. The host of the show will both interview and Socratically question a celebrity. Be sure to inductively outline the Socratic questioning.

Lesson 3
Slippery Slopes and Order Bias

OVERVIEW

This lesson introduces the slippery slope and order bias, two mistakes in the inductive chain of reasoning. The intention is to demonstrate to students that questions can manipulate through emotion and weak reasoning, and compel someone to draw an unwarranted conclusion. There is an absence of analysis and no discovery is made. Students will read or watch an excerpt from the British comedy *Yes, Prime Minister* and discuss its dynamics, comparing and contrasting it with the previously studied excerpts from *Lysis* and *Memorabilia*.

OBJECTIVES

The students will:
- read and understand a passage illustrating order bias,
- understand how emotion can subtly push an argument to avoid examination,
- understand weak induction, and
- better understand the dynamics of Socratic questioning and the role of leading questions.

COMMON CORE STATE STANDARDS

English Language Arts Standards: Reading: Informational Text

Standard 2: Determine a central idea of a text and analyze its development over the course of the text, including its relationship to supporting ideas; provide an objective summary of the text.

Standard 5: Analyze in detail the structure of a specific paragraph in a text, including the role of particular sentences in developing and refining a key concept.

Standard 8: Delineate and evaluate the argument and specific claims in a text, assessing whether the reasoning is sound and the evidence is relevant and sufficient; recognize when irrelevant evidence is introduced.

English Language Arts Standards: Speaking & Listening

Comprehension and Collaboration:

Standard 1a: Come to discussions prepared, having read or researched material under study; explicitly draw on that preparation by referring to evidence on the topic, text, or issue to probe and reflect on ideas under discussion

Standard 3: Delineate a speaker's argument and specific claims, evaluating the soundness of the reasoning and relevance and sufficiency of the evidence and identifying when irrelevant evidence is introduced.

RESOURCES/MATERIALS

- Order Bias text from *Yes, Prime Minister*. It may be possible to find this excerpt on YouTube (http://www.youtube.com). The entire collection of episodes is available on DVD on Amazon (http://www.amazon.com/The-Grand-Design/dp/B0015R516U/ref=sr_1_1?ie=UTF8&qid=1381847017&sr=8-1&keywords=yes%2C+prime+min

ister), where individual episodes may also be purchased for online viewing. The excerpt is from Episode 1, "The Grand Design," of Season 1 (Jay et al., 1986).

PROCEDURE

1. Background
    ▶ *Yes, Prime Minister* is a political satire television series from the 1980s. It shows the antics of a newly elected but inexperienced prime minister who must reckon with a subtle and experienced senior civil servant, Sir Humphrey Appleby.
    ▶ In this episode, the prime minister wishes to bring back the draft, for polls seem to indicate public approval of this action. Believing this to be a terrible error in judgment, Sir Humphrey will seek to undermine the decision by conducting another poll that will find the exact opposite conclusion: The public does not want to bring back the draft. He demonstrates to a colleague how both conclusions can be found through a clever sequence of leading questions. The secret lies in appealing subtly but insistently to a positive emotion.

2. Questions
    ▶ Opening Activity:
        i. Pronounce the word made from this spelling: S –H – O – P. What do you do when you come to a green light? (Many will say "stop"; Myers, 2004, p. 26).
    ▶ Opening Questions
        i. What is happening in this passage?
        ii. What point does Sir Humphrey wish to make?
    ▶ Close Reading/Exploratory
        i. What is a leading question?
            a.) Demonstrate with a short series.
            b.) What are the limitations of leading questions?
            c.) What are the benefits of leading questions?
        ii. How does the method of Sir Humphrey compare to the method of Socrates? (Make a table on the whiteboard.)
            a.) What is the same?
            b.) What is different?
        iii. What issue interests Sir Humphrey? How does he analyze and evaluate it? (He does not.)
        iv. What is moving beneath the questions of Sir Humphrey? What motivates the questions?
            a.) To what emotions does he appeal?
        v. Does Bernard make a discovery in the same way that Lysis and Euthydemus do?
            a.) Does Bernard have a new insight into National Service?
        vi. How does Socrates use leading questions?
        vii. Why does Socrates use questions?

► Concluding
   i. Do you think it is easy to manipulate most people through subtle appeals to emotion? Why? How?
   ii. What is the difference between a conversation and an interview?
   iii. What is the difference between an interview and Socratic questioning?
   iv. What are the benefits and limits of Socratic questioning?

EXTENSION ACTIVITIES

✎ Write a one-page humorous dialogue with a slippery slope argument. Choose an issue from any middle school or high school student's life that could be funny.

✎ Write a one-page dialogue representing a manipulative poll with order bias, in the same manner as Sir Humphrey's. Argue first to one conclusion, then to the opposite conclusion. Be conscious of the emotions to which you appeal (anger, fear, concern, etc.). You may use any issue, but a controversial issue might work best.

✎ In a small group, write a skit about a pollster conducting a manipulative interview who successfully drives another person (or two or three people) to a conclusion, but then the second person (or two or three people) begins to question the pollster Socratically about this conclusion and successfully breaks down the manipulation. The skit can be humorous or serious.

Chapter 6

SEARCHING AND TESTING
Preparing a Socratic Discussion

> It is easier to judge the mind of a man by his questions rather than his answers.
> —Pierre-Marc-Gaston, duc de Lévis

In ancient Athens, educated Greeks cultivated conversation. As we see in the dialogues of Plato, Socrates conversed with anyone in any setting. In the *Symposium*, there is the party following the victory of Agathon, and the group discusses love. In the *Republic*, a group gathers during a religious festival and the conversation centers on justice. Conversation was more reliable than the written word, for if there was a misunderstanding, a lack of clarity, a need to test, you asked a question. You could assert, clarify, analyze, and evaluate. In a word, you could learn.

In the contemporary classroom, discussion is one of the most spontaneous adventures in education. No two discussion groups are alike, no two sessions the same. Each student brings something unique and essential to this group activity that is an opportunity for growth in many ways. In discussion, students become autonomous and critical learners, expressing opinions, listening to others, agreeing or disagreeing for specific motives, searching for clarity, weighing evidence. They have the opportunity to participate in candid exchanges, and to learn tolerance and how to build on one another's contributions.

In this chapter, we look at how to prepare a Socratic discussion. Unlike Socratic dialogue, Socratic discussion is more open in format, so there is more student interaction and less teacher dependence. What is important is to maintain a rhythm of three types of questions: Content, Exploratory, and Analytical. These questions, based upon the categories established by Mortimer Adler for the Great Books discussion groups, keep the discussion grounded in the text, and encourage personal student participation and guide analysis and evaluation (Adler, 1946).

At the same time, as I will address more in the next chapter, Socratic discussion also develops social skills for discussion. The students learn to listen more closely and contribute responsibly to the discussion.

Three Steps

There are three steps in preparation:
1. selecting and preparing the text for specific objectives,
2. drafting the content and exploratory questions as well as the student preparation sheet, and
3. preparing a choice of extension activities.

Planning Step 1: Selection and Preparation of the Text and Objectives

Select texts that have complexity and ambiguity, because these qualities stimulate discussion. A text presenting a controversy compels the students to take a reasoned position on a divergent question, that is, a question with more than one correct answer that must be analyzed and evaluated. The text can be an article in the newspaper, a song, a poem, a short story, a novel, a painting or artwork, a video from the Internet, or a film. Media literacy is more important than ever, and examining advertisements and commercials stimulates lively discussion. Speeches and editorials with a strong position connect to daily life. Contemporary music opens a window to the students' lives and interests. Clearly the text can also come from any subject—history, science, literature, art, mathematics, current events, etc. In selecting it, the basic question is, "Will this text hold the interest of the group and open up authentic and meaningful discussion with different points of view?"

What are the objectives? Bloom's revised taxonomy allows you to articulate precise discussion goals. One can select a single objective or combine them. Will you check for basic understanding? Will you highlight and analyze a particular concept? Will you review a procedure in the course of the discussion? Will you address the formal qualities of the text? Will you ask the students to draw connections to the world today? Do the students have the criteria and standards to evaluate ideas and situations within the text? Will the students confront a complex problem for clarifying and solving as a group?

Preparing the text, whatever its form, requires careful reading and rereading, or viewing and reviewing, as well as brainstorming with your objectives in mind. Is there vocabulary in need of clarification? What are the basic themes and concepts? What are the issues? What are the problems? What is the structure of the argument? Is an outline helpful for understanding structure? Does the text require background information through a multimedia presentation? What are the other possible points of view on the topic?

Reading itself is a conversation with the author. There are famous scribblers of marginalia, such as the Romantic poet William Blake, whose feisty responses in the margins of his books are entertaining and instructive. E-books have made such notemaking easier. For conventional books, there are elaborate methods using signs and symbols, such as the method invented by Mortimer Adler, but one can efficiently abbreviate observations, questions, and summaries without resorting to such a system. Obviously one need not write in the book to make these remarks; I use a notebook and record page numbers.

Planning Step 2: Questions and the Student Preparation Sheet

Socratic questioning develops a heightened awareness of the content and sequencing of questions. In Socratic dialogues, the sequence will be for the most part analytical. An open Socratic discussion, however, will not follow a tight analytical sequence, and in fact there will be fewer questions to prepare. At the same time, a series of open questions is not Socratic, for it invites a wandering discussion and can quickly become an opinion survey and nothing else. Keeping the objectives of the discussion clearly in mind, prepare questions that will achieve those objectives.

In general, the broad structure of the discussion has three parts: (a) a general opening, (b) interpretation and analysis, and (c) summary and extension beyond the classroom.

Before the general opening, at times you may pause to focus the first phase on the retention and understanding of the basic content of the text (the revised taxonomy's first category). The questions determine if all possess an accurate general understanding. You wish to discover and clarify what the author actually said. If the text is theater, film, or fiction, this entails reviewing the characters and events, the setting, unfamiliar vocabulary, chronology and structure, and such, so that it becomes evident everyone has understood what actually has happened before exploring interpretations.

If the text is an essay, this first phase entails reviewing the precise meaning of significant ideas as well as their structure and development. Subject-specific texts such as primary sources in history require clarification of the identity of the author, his or her place in society, purpose in writing, the genre of the text, the intended audience, the question of perspective and bias, the language of the author, and rhetorical devices.

Although personal interpretation must enter into the perception of the text, here you are attempting chiefly to clarify what is the author's own understanding. In many discussions, this stage cannot be skipped, for everyone at the table should begin with the same basic facts and understanding. At times, if the group has not understood the basic content of the text, this phase can lengthen, as Mortimer Adler (1946) observed. But this becomes traditional recitation, and Socratic discussion should go beyond this into application, analysis, and evaluation.

With the basic understanding of the text confirmed, and everyone on the same footing, the general opening of the interpretation and analysis of the text can be broached in different ways.

1. Begin with a student question taken from the Preparation Sheet, an open question that permits extended personal responses. This question can be inspired by a theme of the text, or it can be more general, allowing the students to define the first direction to be explored. There is no right or wrong answer to the question.

   a. What do you think about Sherry Turkle's (2012) belief that increased dependence on technology has damaged human relationships?

2. Break into smaller groups and respond to a thematic question, then report back to the larger group. This can be done in three ways:

   a. Think-Pair-Share (Lyman, 1981): After listening to the question, students think individually about it for a moment, then share and discuss their reflections with a partner. At this point, the pair can unite with another pair for further sharing (this doubling, known as snowballing or pyramiding, can continue), or they can report to the class.

   b. Buzz Groups (Phillips, 1948): J. Donald Phillips pioneered this method of breaking into small groups of six students for 6 minutes of discussion. It became known as Phillips 66. Inform the students when 2 minutes are left, then 1 minute, so that they might attain closure of sorts.

   c. Discussion triads: Separate the students into groups of three. Each student has a role. One becomes the speaker, another the questioner, the third the recorder. The questioner asks the question and seeks clarification or elaboration, and the recorder writes the response and reports to the class. Roles rotate.

3. Discuss a significant quotation from the text. There should be ambiguity, a substantial concept, or a conflict that will generate a variety of responses.

   a. "Law never made men a whit more just; and, by means of their respect for it, even the well-disposed are daily made the agents of injustice."—Henry David Thoreau (1849/1992), *On Civil Disobedience* (p. 669)

   b. "I heartily accept the motto,—'That government is best which governs least'; and I should like to see it acted up to more rapidly and systematically. Carried out, it finally amounts to this, which I also believe,—'That government is best which governs not at all'; and when men are prepared for it, that will be the kind of government which they will have. Government is at best but an expedient; but most governments are usually, and all governments are sometimes, inexpedient."—Henry David Thoreau (1849-1992), *On Civil Disobedience* (p. 667)

4. Do a sentence completion exercise (Brookfield & Preskill, 2005)

   a. The most crucial idea in this reading was . . .

   b. The most confusing part of this film was when . . .

   c. The question I would like to ask the author is . . .

5. Ask the students whether anyone has had a memorable experience similar to the text (Brookfield & Preskill, 2005).

In the second phase, Socratic discussion then explores the meaning of the text by eliciting and analyzing different points of view from the group. Open exploratory questions invite personal responses, and you can start with questions of *why* and *how* (you can also arrive at these analytical questions without using these two words). Then, continue by investigating the reasons for opinions and judgments, by seeking connections, by guiding the application of principles or concepts, or by asking for a prediction of consequences and implications. These follow-up analytical questions seek clarifications and move into the further categories of the revised taxonomy.

By following an exploratory question with analytical questions, students pursue an issue more thoroughly and critically. The students seek clarification of assertions, evidence that supports a position, and they evaluate reasoning. So the rhythm begins with an open question eliciting a personal response, then an analytical question follows, and this alternating of exploring and analyzing continues. Moving spontaneously from participant to participant, comparing and contrasting and linking responses, the discussion quickly takes on a life of its own. There is a sharing of personal perceptions and a continuing analysis.

You can readily recognize the utility of this rhythm. If you removed exploratory questions, the entire personal dimension of the discussion is quashed. On the other hand, if you focused only on such open questions, the personal interpretations of students would be highlighted, but perhaps these interpretations would not be adequately founded on the text, or perhaps there would be inconsistencies as well as unforeseen and undesirable consequences. Recitation of basic content does not engage the students sufficiently at a personal level or analyze the content. Analytical questions alone would render the discussion abstract and disconnected from the students. An alternating rhythm moves the discussion forward, keeping it relevant, personal, and analytical.

The role of the teacher in the discussion will vary according to the objectives as well as the experience and expertise of the student group. As the year progresses, the skills of the students should become sharper and the leading role of the teacher diminish. In some discussions there may be no need for any teacher intervention after the initiation.

How many questions are necessary? Four or five exploratory questions will be sufficient for an hour, given that each question will stimulate extended conversation. Eight to 10 questions will be more than enough. Write the questions as simply and clearly as possible. They should not be small paragraphs or have abstract or abstruse language. Keep in mind that the questions may have to be clarified during the discussion.

The Student Preparation Sheet

It is a common experience to attend a meeting at which new information is presented. We listen, we watch the multimedia presentation, but at the break for questions and discussion, we hesitate to participate because we have not yet come to terms with what we think and feel. We are unsure if we remember the points correctly. We have not had the opportunity to reflect. A few individuals who are self-confident and verbally quick offer their opinions, and the discussion slides along with impressionistic remarks from a minority of those present. But it does not attain sufficient breadth and depth.

Classes can be like this for students: Confronted with new material, they are not sure of their thoughts and feelings about it, and a few vocal students dominate discussion. The student preparation sheet (p. 140) is of paramount importance because it gives all of the students the opportunity to reflect upon their thoughts and feelings toward the text and so arrive at an articulate personal understanding before entering discussion. In discussion, we do not want a quick duel of opinions, with the strongest personality triumphant, but a reasonably paced cooperative examination. If students have already discovered their own thoughts and reactions, then the discussion begins on more solid ground for them. The emphasis in discussion shifts to the skills of shared examination. Their own thoughts and feelings can be thrown into relief by those of other students.

Given a few days before the discussion, the preparation sheet presents the basic facts and understandings as well as selected exploratory questions that will be pursued (see p. 42). The final question on the sheet can always be, What did you find difficult or confusing? It is likely there will be a pattern in responses, allowing for discussion of precisely that aspect of the text.

The preparation sheet permits students to foresee the broad arc of the conversation, and so be able to prepare their own points, explanations, and examples. They have the chance to sort out their feelings and thoughts about the topic. They can also prepare their own questions.

For this, teach the students about open and closed questions and how to focus questions with Bloom's revised taxonomy. Asking the students to submit questions the day before discussion invites and stimulates their participation. They can moreover indicate what they found particularly difficult or confusing, and this can greatly clarify your own preparation.

Planning Step 3: An Extending Activity

The final phase of the discussion answers the question, *What will the students take away?* Summarizing allows students to reflect on the form and content of the discussion. But it would be counterproductive for the teacher to sweep the varied remarks into a meaningful whole for the students. Ask the students to select the most significant findings of the discussion and how and why these findings are significant.

How will the students transfer the learning? You need to take the topic beyond the classroom. What you want is not for the students to memorize a new series of correct answers, but to construct valid understandings that can be applied in a personal way to the world around them. The concluding question or activity fosters this transfer of learning.

Nearly 20 years ago, Robert J. Sternberg and Elena L. Grigorenko (2004) suggested in a theory of successful intelligence that we each possess overlapping analytic, practical, and creative intelligence. Different cultures in the world place emphasis on one or another of these forms, and individuals themselves will have strengths and weaknesses. Using this insight concerning successful intelligence, which aligns very well with Bloom's taxonomy, one can give a choice of activities to the students to foster more personal engagement. For example:

- Write an argumentative essay about the ethics of testing cosmetics on animals. (Analytic)
- Write a persuasive speech for or against testing on animals. (Analytic)
- Write an article for the school newspaper on animal testing. (Analytic)
- Design a community project to raise awareness of animal rights. (Practical)
- Organize a walk for animal rights. (Practical)
- Lobby local, state, or federal politicians for animal rights. (Practical)
- Make a short film about animals used in cosmetic testing. (Creative)
- Write a story about an animal subjected to animal testing. (Creative)
- Write a story about a person who benefits from a drug or a medical procedure perfected through animal testing. (Creative)

Even better, one can also allow students to brainstorm and formulate their own activity along these lines.

How Should the Class Sit?

One indispensable means of fostering cohesion in the group is to rearrange the desks or chairs. Every classroom setup expresses a teaching philosophy. Breaking the template of the traditional classroom, whose desks and chairs are arranged in neat rows focused on the teacher's desk, has a powerful effect on classes. Robert Chambers (2009) observed that "Seating arrangements carry coded messages about relationships. They put us in positions ranged between disciplined and chaotic, formal and informal, centralized and decentralized, hierarchical and egalitarian, exposed and private, and threatening and non-threatening" (p. 83). There is a palpable change in classroom atmosphere when the teacher-centered arrangement of furniture changes. In seeing itself, the group recognizes itself and becomes a group.

What are the possible configurations? Students can sit in a circle, a half circle, a U, a hollow square, in triangles, or in two concentric circles (fishbowl). The "fishbowl" arrangement, made more popular through Socratic circles, has one circle on the inside that discusses the text while the circle outside critically observes and evaluates the discussion. The drawback of this popular arrangement is that the outer circle essentially is passive in its observation and can easily become bored. Boredom in turn can lead to behavior problems. One solution is to shift the observers to the inner circle after 10 minutes.

Conclusion

A final step, whenever possible, is to discuss the lesson plan with a colleague during common planning time. Is the text appropriate? Are the objectives realistic? Are the questions appropriately phrased and directed for those objectives? Are the extension activities appropriately varied and challenging?

Review your preparation the night before teaching, and in the morning before going to school or entering the classroom. The ideas should be fresh. The emphasis in the classroom is on active listening and appropriate response to the students in the effort to develop skills in thinking and in group discussion, so you do not want to be chained to a question sheet. The objectives as well as the fundamental questions should be clear in your head, or you can familiarize yourself with them at a glance.

Chapter 7

SPLITTING THE EDUCATION ATOM
Conducting a Socratic Discussion

> Once you have learned how to ask questions—relevant and appropriate and substantial questions—you have learned how to learn and no one can keep you from learning whatever you want or need to know . . .
> —Neil Postman and Charles Weingartner

The word *discussion* is derived from the Latin verb *discutere*, to shatter, to break apart. Everyone knows that discussion can explode a topic in unforeseen directions, and for many, this can be a source of disorientation and frustration. But discussion splits the education atom, and in its energy we discover valuable new perspectives. In Socratic discussion, the teacher seeks to guide and facilitate this effort, keeping it relevant and open. You foster engagement by preparing the students for the experience, by creating a climate of psychological safety and trust for participation, and by conducting the discussion with patience and kindness. In this way, the students not only develop a more nuanced and personal understanding of the topic, but they also develop important skills in listening, thinking, and speaking.

Discussion is a delicate and complex activity, requiring not only emotional intelligence as well as intellectual skills for effective leadership. Leadership has generated a great deal of interesting scholarship. One early theory, derived from the study of the interaction of children, divides leadership into three styles, autocratic, democratic, and laissez-faire. The autocrat dominates the group entirely, demanding obedience and compliance. For the autocrat, speaking out of turn may be an act of insubordination more than a symptom of lack of skills. Laissez-faire leadership, on the other hand, grants greatest freedom to the group, but if the group does not have the necessary focus, skills, and spirit of cooperation, confusion ensues. The group dissolves and its objectives will not be met. Democratic leadership takes a middle course, making clear expectations and goals, inviting participation, and sharing responsibility. Kurt Lewin (Lewin, Lippit, & White, 1939) discovered that democratic leadership was the most effective style.

Different groups of students will need different styles of leadership. Students who have not developed the requisite skills and maturity will need more guidance from the teacher, and you will assume a more autocratic style to maintain order and guide the students to progress. You must lead the students to develop the skills for democratic discussion. Students who have developed the skills will need less guidance, and you can justifiably and necessarily become more laissez-faire in style because the students know what they are doing. You grant the students the time and space for autonomous growth. Every group will be different, some days may be better than others, and you can find your leadership style more often in a continuum between the three poles. In the best of cases, you want to bring the students to the self-sufficiency and self-reliance that means you can be laissez-faire and they are democratic.

Democratic discussion is among the most important cooperative activities in school. By modeling and fostering a democratic style of leadership, we invite students to participate responsibly and respectfully. The students become the creators of the discussion, and continue to develop thinking and social skills that immediately transfer to life beyond the classroom.

Guidelines for Participation

Democratic discussion steers a middle course between the formal and the informal. The basic guidelines are simple and explicit. Too many guidelines will be hard to remember and will make the class a martial exercise.

1. Prepare for the discussion.
2. Know what you think and feel about the topic.
3. Listen actively and respectfully.
4. Disagreement is welcome, but we all must be civil and kind.

The guidelines are very important to make explicit and discuss. Students must feel and understand that there is a safe environment for personal disclosure. This means that there cannot be irony or sarcasm at someone's expense, or whispering in private conversations, or making odd facial expressions, like rolling the eyes. One person must speak at a time, and no one should interrupt another speaker, especially in disagreement. There is never a need to shout. Particularly in the first sessions, it is necessary to teach and make absolutely clear these four expectations and their motivation. They help create an atmosphere of inclusion, tolerance, and support. If there is no preparation and respect, and students do not understand the specific behaviors that express respect, the discussion will not go far. Within the guidelines, there is greater freedom of expression and communication.

The overall classroom management plan, which every teacher should have, will delineate consequences for transgression of the guidelines. Lighter offenses can be corrected with eye contact, a mild gesture, or a gentle word. More disruptive behavior needs more direct intervention. Consequences can take a variety of forms, from separation within the classroom to sending to the office. It is always best to speak with students privately, maintaining a calm tone. The student should reflect on the disruption, what caused it, and how to avoid the impulse to disrupt in the future.

With the guidelines communicated, students will nonetheless bring the expectations and behavior for discussion from those conducted in other classes at school. In other classrooms, discussions may be strictly authoritarian, with the expectation that the teacher's point of view be unquestioningly accepted; in still other classrooms, the discussions may be laissez-faire romps, with individual students becoming unrestrainedly emotional, shouting at each other, teasing, taunting. Quickly setting the democratic tone and form in your own classroom is important.

Looks Like, Sounds Like, Feels Like

To reinforce the idea of democratic discussion in the classroom, one can fill out the chart in Figure 12 on a large poster. It is a simple exercise, but effective for focusing on the important ideas. Do another version with a collage of pictures. Hang the poster up in the front of the classroom as a year-long reminder.

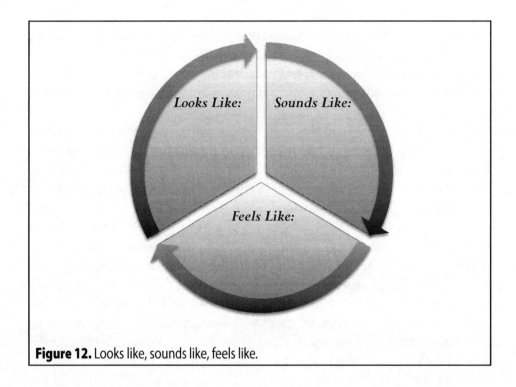

Figure 12. Looks like, sounds like, feels like.

Democratic Discussion: Group Building

Recently I accompanied a group of students to a Model United Nations conference. For many students there, it was their first conference. The students came from many different nations, and for the majority, English was not their first language. On the first day, as I sat in a classroom to observe an opening session, the students seemed tense, nervous, and anxious. Then the student leader of the commission affably introduced himself, spoke of his experience with Model United Nations, and cheerfully shared with the students, "My favorite color is purple and my favorite animal, the panda." He then invited all of the delegates in the room to introduce themselves and to share their favorite color and animal. As student after student shared, the tension diminished. A simple exercise, the icebreaker had a palpable effect on the room and the session moved ahead in a more relaxed manner.

Any class is a small community that reunites regularly. Some students have perhaps known each other since nursery school, while others may have arrived in September or only the day before. Class discussion takes place within this small community. If the community is accepting and comfortable with itself, the experience will be positive, and the community will cooperate in an open and nonthreatening manner. One can foster greater acceptance and comfort through different activities, such as icebreakers, perhaps the most underrated and neglected element of group preparation.

What are examples of effective ice-breaking activities? Here are four:

1. My neighbor is . . . (Bond, 1990). Divide the students into pairs. For 10 minutes, the students take turns interviewing each other about their life and interests (5 minutes each). As one student recounts, the interviewer takes notes. At the end of 10 minutes, each student presents her neighbor.

2. Detective (Bond, 1990). Divide the students into pairs who do not know each other and have each pair take out a pen and paper. Without explaining or speaking at all, each student must draw six objects they have used in the last 3 months. These objects must allow the other person to discover something important about themselves (e.g, a swimmer might draw a swimming pool). After both students have finished drawing, each tries to guess what the drawings reveal about the other person. At the end of the activity, the partners reveal what they have learned through their detective work.

3. Categories (Brandes, 1990b). All of the students sit in a circle. A leader calls out the names of groups (e.g., music lovers, online game players, bloggers, basketball players, Justin Bieber fans, etc). People who belong to the group move to the center of the circle. Another group is called out. If the students belong to this group, they remain; otherwise they return to their place in the circle. Brainstorm categories beforehand.

4. Absent Friends (Brandes, 1990b). Students sit in a circle. Ask them: "Who is the next person you would like to see coming through the door and what would you like to say to them?" The person can be anyone—a friend, a celebrity, a fictional person, a family member.

Other icebreakers are effective in acquainting students. To a large degree, they depend on the comfort level of the teacher and group. Some teachers would use icebreakers I would not, and certainly the reverse is true as well. Some undoubtedly would not be appropriate in a smaller classroom with encumbering furniture. Many can be found online (search the word "icebreakers"), and there are many books with collections (e.g., Ragsdale & Saylor, 2007; West, 1999). They introduce an element of fun and entertainment that will dissolve the solemnity and formality that can surround academic discussions. Do icebreakers throughout the year. The process of the group coming together only really ends with the last class.

Leading the Discussion

Begin the discussion with the clear statement of the topic and objectives. What are we talking about and why are we talking about it? All of the students should know the goals of the discussion. Then, lead from the prepared outline of questions. You can foresee approximately 10 to 15 minutes of discussion for each exploration question, although there is no absolute rule. For students in middle school or the first years of high school, it is effective to change direction every 15 minutes in order to maintain interest.

The class itself determines the pace and direction of the discussion. Basic questions review content that must be shared, but exploratory questions determine the personal understanding of the students, then analytical questions closely examine this understanding. The larger rhythm of basic, exploratory, and analytical questions moves through the discussion. Searching and testing are what give the discussion its Socratic character.

Follow-up questions gently prod the discussion to keep momentum and relevancy. Besides the questions specifically formulated for the discussion, follow-up questions help students to develop and explore their thoughts, as shown in Figure 5 on p. 63.

Silence is always helpful. Do not hurry to cover it with a nervous stream of words. It may be that you must rephrase your question to make it more open or more approachable. Creating an accepting atmosphere coaxes the students into contributing.

You can also choreograph a soft conflict by eliciting one perspective, then asking if anyone has a different view (as Michael Sandel does so skillfully with his students at Harvard). With two opposing views in the open, begin to question each side for the assumptions and consequences of their positions. Ask each person to react to the other. Do more people in the group agree with one side? Is there still another perspective?

In the best cases, as mentioned above, the class discussion will take on a life of its own. Students will spontaneously share their thoughts and opinions, constructively interacting with the other students. There will be clarifications, challenges, and connections. Many will participate. There will be no excessively heated debates. The teacher will be able to observe the discussion and make notes. But students must develop a complex set of skills to achieve this degree of autonomy.

The first skill is listening. Listening well is very challenging for everyone. We are moving fast. The shift of gears from other classes, which require other kinds of work, can be demanding on both students and teacher alike. Students may be coming from physical education classes, or science labs, or a test. Listening, however, is an indispensable skill. For if there is no listening, there is no discussion. We listen not only for content, but for nuances, new ideas, attitudes, emotions, and feelings. In listening, we observe facial expressions, gestures, and body language. We listen to affirm the importance of the other person and what he or she says. We exercise emotional intelligence.

Daniel Goleman (1996) has popularized the notion of emotional intelligence. He identified five aspects: self-awareness, managing emotions, motivation, empathy, and social skills. All of these aspects come into play for every participant in a discussion. Teachers and students develop more self-awareness, and they must manage their emotions, using restraint when encountering a point of view with which they passionately disagree. They must make an emotional bridge to the other person through empathy and cross it through their social skills.

As I said in the previous chapter, controversy is not bad. In fact, it increases learning, for one is driven to examine the motives and assumptions for basic commitments. But before confronting an especially controversial topic, one can review the four guidelines with the class, underlining the need to listen actively and respectfully. It is a bad idea to raise the voice, for we begin to react to the emotion and not to the idea. At times, there is a crescendo from polite earnestness to outspoken exasperation. Expect flare-ups and recognize them as learning opportunities for the entire class. Students will be working on managing emotions, and you need tactics to slow and cool the discussion. One excellent method, used in Quaker meetings, is to impose a long pause of a few minutes so that emotional equilibrium is reestablished.

Another skill for the leader is more difficult to acquire and hone. Be funny, at least sometimes. Depending on the topic of discussion, humor often brings a welcome gust of joy and entertainment. It is cathartic, releasing pent-up tension or emotion. What Shakespeare does with the Porter scene in Macbeth has its application in the classroom (with less vulgarity!). Studies have shown that humor increases learning at all levels of education (Minchew & Hopper, 2008; Torok, McMorris, & Lin, 2004). Some teachers and students are naturally funny, spontaneously discovering the appropriate comic insight and phrase within any situation. Fun is an important element of teaching; otherwise the class period takes on unrelenting seriousness, and day after day of serious discussion becomes boring. Without having a natural gift for comedy, one can consciously bring humor into the discussion by finding the comic anecdote that fits the topic or issue.

Although student discussion preparation is indispensable, and the discussion does need to have a point, I believe that discussions should be as open as possible. Guidance or facilitation is necessary, but this does not mean the imposition of a point of view or a "correct answer." In turn, this does not imply that every point of view is equally valid, only that each point of view can equally be considered and analyzed for validity. If an autocratic teacher is swatting opinions down like so many flies, the students learn to be quiet, without changing their minds. They know they have to repeat the teacher's answer on the test. Many students, abandoning completely the need to think, will reflexively learn to ask the bottom-line academic survival question, "What is the right answer?"

Socrates' refusal to give answers is very wise. Answer questions with questions. Redirect the question to other students. In most discussions, I prefer the students not know what I think.

Recognizing contributions is important as well, but this should be done without conditioning the students to believe you are simply affirming your own point of view expressed by a student. Although there are educationists who eschew rewarding (and blaming) students, I believe that honestly praising students is very important, for it instantly and visibly increases self-esteem. There are students who have been conditioned by teachers and peers for years to believe they are less intelligent, creative, and insightful. They dread being in class. Praise turns that perception around. Praise encourages the students to see themselves in a new light. You can see facial expressions change and body language alter with a newfound self-esteem.

The students should be doing most of the talking. Resist any urge to comment at length upon an answer or to begin a minilecture. It may be necessary to coordinate the contributions more evenly. One student or a small group of students should not dominate the discussion. A fixed pattern of sharing should be disrupted, because it excludes others. This may mean altering the seating in the circle, and moving students around to break patterns.

Observation and Recording the Socratic Discussion

Observing the dynamics of the discussion is a major task for the leader. You must discern the individual strengths and weaknesses of each participant in order to bring that person forward in his or her skills. Recording the pattern of discussion is important. There is more than one method to record the discussion pattern. One method is to make an interaction chart like the one in Figure 13. (Don't forget to put yourself on the chart!)

Recording the discussion with a video camera is an excellent method. Tell the students you will record the conversation to improve your own skills in discussion leadership. Students in most cases quickly forget the camera and the discussion continues. You will learn a great deal about yourself as a teacher.

Assessment

As a teacher, you have three fundamental tasks: planning, guiding, and evaluation. You have planned and guided the discussion, and now you must evaluate the entire experience. Evaluation is important for everyone's progress, the teacher included. How does one assess a Socratic discussion?

First, evaluate whether the objectives of the discussion have been attained. A chart such as that shown in Figure 14 can be very helpful in your evaluation. Were the students prepared? Has there been critical thinking? Has there been problem solving? Has there been progress in the specific objectives? What contributions are evidence of this? What did the students take away?

Don't forget to also assess the development of discussion social skills. Has there been an atmosphere of support? Has there been encouragement through active listening?

Reflecting on the discussion in a teaching journal is an absolute necessity. This will help you to understand better the contributions of individual students and especially your own responses, what went well, and what can be improved.

Share the individual assessments with the students privately. Share the group assessment collectively. At the end of the period, debrief the discussion from the viewpoint of skills development. Ask the students for their impressions and judgments. What has gone better? What needs more work? Have needs and issues been uncovered for futher discussion? This is seizing the opportunity for growth in metacognition.

Mr. Wilberding	Jacob	Aiden	Abigail	Mary	Judy	Julia	Anthony	Javier	Achmed	Beatrice	Sophia
Mr. Wilberding											
Jacob											
Aiden											
Abigail											
Mary											
Julia											
Anthony											
Javier											
Achmed											
Beatrice											
Sophia											

Figure 13. Interaction chart.

	Preparation	Active Listening	Contributions	Questions
Mr. Wilberding				
Jacob				
Aiden				
Abigail				
Mary				
Julia				
Anthony				
Javier				
Achmed				
Beatrice				
Sophia				

Figure 14. Evaluation chart.

Improving Discussion Skills

Generally, students must be taught to discuss democratically. Even articulate and self-confident students can refine their skills in listening to others and taking into account other perspectives. Many students are reticent at the beginning. Most can be coaxed from their shells when they realize there is no danger. The motives for lack of participation can be multifold. Lack of preparation is one common motive. A student may feel awkward in self-expression, or fearful about speaking in a group. There may be a conflicting relationship with another student in the classroom. A student may simply find the material boring and irrelevant (which may make you search for more explicit connections or change your material!). A student may have a personal problem outside of school. Some motives can be beyond the reach of the teacher, requiring the gentle and discreet intervention of the school psychologist.

Another reason why discussion can slow is that the entire experience of open discussion is foreign to the students. In their scholastic lives, and perhaps in their lives at home, they have been conditioned to be quiet and passively obedient, not vocal and constructively critical. They are waiting for direction so that they can do the right thing and be approved. They perceive the adult as the expert and believe their duty is to listen. They also fear for their grades. Students are quick to perceive boundary lines and to understand that a teacher wishes his or her own view assimilated and repeated. They have not learned that they and their peers have worthwhile thoughts and feelings.

Besides great music, the 1960s and 1970s produced some wonderful and worthwhile approaches to discussion teaching. Published in 1969, *Learning Discussion Skills Through Games* by Gene Stanford and Barbara Dodds Stanford is small treasury of fun activities for developing skills. In a later book, Gene Stanford developed and expanded further insights and reflections, fitting them within a five-stage theoretical model of student group development (1977). Both books are wonderful resources for understanding and developing democratic skills in the classroom. I have taken the following five games from the book published in 1969, modifying them slightly at times and using different issues. For other games, you can consult Bond (1990) as well as Brandes (1990a, 1990b).

Taking Responsibility to Contribute

Each student in the classroom has something to share in the discussion. This activity encourages students to step forward to say something constructive. Divided into small groups, the students sit in circles. There is a question for them to answer, and it is a question for which everyone will have an answer. For example:

- What is the best video game?
- Who is the best singer or musical group now?
- What is the best app?
- What is the best movie?

Each student in the circle must contribute an answer, and the answers must be given in a *random* order, that is, the answers cannot be given clockwise or counterclockwise. The group whose members answer the question first, in the random order, wins the game.

Following the game, there can be a brief period of sharing to discover how each group encouraged reticent members to speak.

Responding to Others

In classroom discussions, at times it can be difficult to link contributions effectively. The session can become opinion sharing, with one opinion following another, but without a reflective consideration of the ideas shared by other members of the group. In a good discussion, people are not talking past each other. This activity cultivates the habit of responding to other members of the group.

An open question is given to the group (small or large). "Should the school have a uniform?" "Does the excessive use of cell phones harm human relationships?" "Are movies more important than books?" Ask one student to give an opinion. Then call on another student to respond to the first speaker. The second speaker must look at the first student, paraphrase what was said, and tell the group whether she agrees or disagrees and how. Then a third student does the same for the second student, and so on.

Careful Listening

Debates can ignite within discussion, particularly when examining controversial issues, and at times, there are groups that will have participants who will swerve the discussion into an argument, in this way quashing the open atmosphere that encourages greater and more constructive participation. Some classes will have their antagonists who predictably clash in every discussion. To prevent the group from collapsing in this way, the following activity is helpful.

Select a controversial issue:

- Should junk food be banned from schools?
- Should the Internet be censored?
- Should animal testing be banned?
- Should university education be free?
- Should beauty contests be banned?
- Should the sale of guns be more controlled?

Select a student to express an opinion on this issue. Then another student must paraphrase this contribution and then articulate to what extent he agrees with it. He cannot simply disagree. He must clearly understand the other person's point of view and discover agreement to some extent. Once this is done, then the second student can give his own point of view more fully, telling why and how he disagrees with the first (if this is the case). Then a third student is selected for the paraphrasing and response, and then a fourth student, and so on.

Encouraging Contribution

Competition can infiltrate and quickly permeate discussions. Competition can hurtle into argument, and arguments can become inflamed. Although differences of opinion are important to acknowledge and investigate, argument that becomes head-butting should be avoided.

Gene Stafford suggests an interpersonal issue for this activity. An excellent resource for such issues or problems is *The Kids' Book of Questions* by Gregory Stock (2004). In this book, there are 268 questions, some of which might not be helpful in an academic setting. But many are, including the following.

- What is the hardest thing about growing up? (p. 50)
- If you could change any one thing about the way you look, what would it be? (p. 72)
- Are you afraid to ask questions when you don't understand something? For example, do you sometimes fake a laugh when you do not understand a joke? (p. 73)

Before beginning a discussion, write on the board different possible empathetic responses to what will be said. The speaker cannot express his own views, but must try to draw the other person out through careful listening. There can be no argument. Possible empathetic responses include:

- asking questions for more information,
- expressions of support,
- requests for clarification,
- rephrasing what the speaker says or feels, and
- offering personal examples of the same experiences.

The group then observes two students carry out this nonjudgmental discussion. Students can break into twos to continue this activity.

Learning New Roles

Students can become fixed in patterns of interaction. This activity explores roles that students can play within discussion, which include the following:

- Initiator
  - ▷ Starts the discussion
  - ▷ Introduces new ideas
  - ▷ Raises new questions
- Clarifier
  - ▷ Asks for more information
  - ▷ Requests definitions of vague terms
- Summarizer
  - ▷ Points out areas of agreement and disagreement
  - ▷ Indicates where the group stands on the issue
- Evaluator
  - ▷ Observes the process of discussion and determines strengths and weaknesses in the process.

The teacher writes the roles on small slips of paper (Initiator, Clarifier, Summarizer, Evaluator, Contributing Group Member) and distributes them to students, who cannot tell others the role they have received. When the discussion finishes, the students should guess who played each role.

Conclusion

There are other kinds of discussion. One can problem solve, build consensus, or make collective decisions after the thoughful consideration of alternatives with their assumptions and consequences. Edward De Bono's Six Thinking Hats method is marvelously effective for organizing groups to think constructively in parallel. A Socratic discussion is directed to developing cognitive as well as personal and social skills. It is not a meeting of minds, but the gathering of a small community of learners.

The most influential aspect of discussion is the tone of the environment. If all of the students feel genuinely respected and comfortable, then they will share authentically. They will disclose personal opinions and convictions. If there is an adversarial atmosphere, or if they feel that dissenters will be punished and loyalists rewarded, then a submissive exercise will take place. An aggressive or dystopian classroom shuts down authentic discussion, and students do not learn democratic skills that are important to the community.

Mortimer J. Adler (1946) once wrote that there are no perfect discussions. There is always more to be said, which is often true. One must be selective in objectives and assess the discussion rigorously in those terms. As with Socratic dialogues, it is important to reflect on the experience for improvement. Discussion needs its place within the curriculum in all subjects for students to assimilate its democratic habits.

Chapter 8

CONCLUSION
Thinking and Arguing Together

Between the two World Wars, a new form of art education was born at the Bauhaus in Germany. Up to that time, artists learned largely through close imitation. They imitated by copying drawings or plaster casts. At the Bauhaus, however, there was a new philosophy of education: Teachers would teach the elements and principles of art, and then the students would freely apply them to new modern materials. This new philosophy engendered an outpouring of creativity in all directions. The Bauhaus left its mark in painting, sculpture, and architecture, but also in industrial design in countless ways that are still seen in objects from toys to teapots to typography. What Florence was to the Renaissance, the Bauhaus was to the 20th century. City skylines and children's playrooms still show its creative and highly intelligent influence.

Socratic teaching similarly requires learning the adaptable elements and versatile principles of the Socratic Method and applying them freely, creatively, and intelligently in new contexts. It is challenging and requires a complex set of skills, but it is particularly relevant in the rapidly changing 21st-century. Critical thinking that examines the bases and structure of arguments is crucial as never before. As Vernor Vinge and Raymond Kurzweil, among others, have pointed out, technological change happens at an exponential pace. There is no plateau or stasis. Adaptation to the steep curve of development is a key skill, and critical-creative thinking is required. Democratic collaboration is required.

Broadly applied, focused upon problems and open questions, Socratic learning becomes the discovery learning advocated today by many educationists. In more strictly dialogic form, differentiated to the class and the individual student, it is challenging for teacher and student alike because, although planned, it nonetheless is fluid in its execution and so requires agility. As the critical principles are awoken in the student, the Socratic exploration becomes more and more shared. As Paolo Freire (1996) wrote,

> Through dialogue, the teacher-of-the students and the students-of-the-teacher cease to exist and a new term emerges: teacher-student with students-teachers . . . [together they] become jointly responsible for a process in which all grow. (p. 61)

But Socratic teaching is not simply dialogic teaching. It is not a discussion or interview. There is an inductive movement from particulars to a generalization or conclusion, an insistent critical movement to discovery. As Pólya observed, "What is good education? Giving systematically opportunity to the student to discover things by himself" (Polya & Szego, 1972/1998, p. vi). The Socratic dialogue and discussion provide such a systematic opportunity for discovery.

The Socratic dialogues of Plato and Xenophon are classics of discovery pedagogy. They are not only literary creations, but glimpses of the first open and democratic classroom, the agora of Athens. Although we can no longer see how Polygnotus drew and layered his paintings of the Taking of Troy, or how Phidias carved a marble sculpture of Athena, we can just barely hear over such a great distance how Socrates practiced his art of education with its unique tools, questions, and analogies. Socrates was not the perfect teacher, and 5th century Athens was not a perfect society. But he was on to something that remains relevant. He taught for understanding and authenticity. Such inductive questioning will always have a place in learning to think critically.

An Age of Paraphrasing?

Contemporary students are confronted with a vast amount of information, and the only limitations are imposed by their skills and curiosity. Left to themselves and harried by deadlines, students may move information from the computer screen to a printed page without thinking, and then dart to the next assignment. The keys to their limited learning become *ctlr*, *c*, and *p*, just enough to cut and paste. They can make the Web quests, conduct quick raids on online resources like Wikipedia or more specialized websites, but they do not know what to do with the information besides summarize and present it. They cannot analyze, evaluate, or create. They do not examine the bases, or foresee the implications or consequences. Left to themselves, they gather the ore and display it, but they do not know how to recognize, separate, and refine the metal or how to make something beautiful and useful with it.

The Socratic Method leads the students beyond such paraphrasing, which represents at its best the Understanding category of Bloom's taxonomy. Paraphrasing does represent a degree of understanding, but is not far from rote learning. Through Socratic learning, the students move from information-gathering to knowledge production. In a Socratic classroom, one cannot rest with paraphrasing. The Socratic instinct is to explore and investigate together. What makes the experience especially challenging for the teacher is the necessity to think well. *In primis* the teacher must think critically, understanding the key concept or process thoroughly, then know how to guide the student down the path of analysis and evaluation with the appropriate questions, analogies, and examples, leaving the student aware and well-equipped at the gateway of creativity.

Why Use the Socratic Method?

Critical and creative thinking takes different directions in different subjects. That is, critical and creative thinking will take one form in the natural sciences and others in art or mathematics or in literature classes. For instance, the scientific method, which is the sequenced process of observation, hypothesis, and testing, will not usually be taught in composition classes. Formal analysis of paintings will lead to more suggestive artistic interpretations, sometimes very personal interpretations, than generally are possible in mathematics classes, where deductive thinking rigorously leads to a single correct answer on the other side of the equals sign. All of these fields create knowledge by different methods.

And yet, the two Socratic methods offer guidelines to teaching in all of these fields. One is teaching for deeper understanding, and this at every moment prevents the teacher from going on autopilot. You must be engaged with the students, and the teacher and the students must be focused on the questions. Done poorly, the questioning is vague and unfocused, or autocratic and unbending. Such questioning is not genuinely Socratic. Done well, Socratic questioning is antiauthoritarian and nonconformist, not accepting statements without analysis, evaluation, and application, not accepting anything without understanding.

The colorful, controversial, and pragmatic Saul Alinsky, in a conversation with Studs Terkel (n.d.), recounted what might happen if a labor organizer arrived at the Oracle of Delphi and heard the command, "Know yourself." The practical organizer would respond, "Okay Oracle, now how do I go about doing it? Don't tell me what I have to get, tell me how I have to get it because unless I know the 'how' the 'what' is just rhetoric you know" (para. 7).

The Socratic Method is the *how*. Through inductive questioning, the teacher facilitates the deeper understanding of claims, premises, issues, and problems. By verbally guiding critical thinking, the teacher draws the student forward, which is the core meaning of the word *education*. The paradigm of *I do, We do, You do* frames the Socratic experience. Beginning with *We do*, the teacher gives enough help without giving too much, so that the student passes to *You do*, autonomous performance. Socratic Method navigates the space between *we do* and *I do*. The inductive outline is the beginning, but one must expect and be ready to depart from the outline to bring the students forward.

Two extraordinary aspects of the Socratic Method are its adaptability and flexibility. Already this is visible in the works of Plato and Xenophon, as well as in the modern adaptations to elementary, legal, and business education, but in middle and high school one can adapt the Socratic Method to achieve different learning objectives in different subjects in both the sciences and the humanities. One can inductively lead students to concept attainment, to the application of principles and rules in new situations, through the process of analysis and evaluation.

The importance of learning how to think critically and creatively, how to argue (in the best sense of this word; i.e., how to construct arguments), and how to collaborate cannot be overestimated. These skills form the basis of democracy. The founding fathers were philosophers, their words carefully chosen and arguments skillfully made, and many had read the dialogues of Plato and Xenophon. Like most 18th-century readers, they preferred Xenophon. Thomas Jefferson very strongly disliked Plato (who dealt out "mysticisms incomprehensible to the human mind") and recommended Xenophon to students (Wright, 1943, p. 229). In his *Autobiography*, Benjamin Franklin wrote about an early and somewhat mischievous enthusiasm for Socratic dialogue, learned through reading Xenophon, which left a lasting mark on his manner of thinking and contributed to forming his gentle and nonconfrontational way of persuading others (Houston, 2004).

Democracy thrives on informed and critical argument, which should be learned in school. Specifically citing Socrates and his habit of intensive questioning, Martha C. Nussbaum (2010) recently discussed the importance of critical thinking to preserve a vibrant democracy, arguing for the qualitative approach of Socratic education over the more impersonal quantitative approach measured through standardized testing, part of a business climate that increasingly impacts American education. Critical thinking leads to clarity about goals and how to achieve them. It makes meaningful political debate in society possible. Impervious to peer pressure, it also is the tool by which democratic society dispels the enchantment of a charismatic individual who peddles mere rhetoric.

Socratic education also meticulously examines claims, concepts, issues, and problems that many today, in a pluralistic society or global village, might refrain from criticizing in the spirit of relativism. The relativist believes that the truth of any matter will vary according to the society and culture, perhaps even according to the individual. What is true for you, the relativist asserts, may not be true for me.

Although it is easy to demonstrate a variety of opinions on myriad matters, and to assert and teach that one ought to respect opinions, this does not excuse an individual from critical examination and judgment of the opinions themselves. For the Socratic learner, there is no passive acceptance that everyone has their own point of view. The default conviction is that often we think we know, but we probably have not yet thought about it seriously. And it is often effective to think about it seriously by engaging others in dialogue and discussion.

The Socratic Method can be applied to any subject, but the topic of ethics continues to be fertile ground for discussion. Robert J. Sternberg (2013) is one advocate of teaching ethics in school, Howard Gardner (2006) another. Students need to understand how to approach ethical questions in their personal lives as well as in the dynamic discussions that confront a rapidly changing society. A participatory democracy requires competence in understanding and discussing these far-reaching issues and principles.

For this analysis and evaluation, the Socratic Method provides inductive guidance in clear steps appropriate to the individual and group.

Designing the Steps

Staircases in Rome provide a good analogy for teaching with questions. In particular, three staircases offer an analogy. On the Capitoline Hill stands the church of Santa Maria in Aracoeli, a grand medieval basilica before which is a very long staircase made after the Black Plague in the 14th century. There are 128 steps driving up a steep angle to the door of the church. It is a strenuous climb, not one that is repeated often, unless you have a special interest in urban training for mountain trekking. It is a penitential climb.

Not far from this is the more graduated staircase, or *cordonata*, leading to the square designed by Michelangelo in the 16th century. Broad steps at a gentle incline permit a painless ascent into the square. The longer steps once allowed horses and carriages to ascend. Today one arrives to the square without being winded. In fact, most people are conversing as they stroll upwards, aware of the effort but not distracted by it. Most are excited by the discovery they are making as they walk into one of the most celebrated and historical squares in the world.

The third staircase is the celebrated Spanish Steps, designed by an Italian architect for a French patron in the 18th century. Here steps rise to terraces that make the climbing more leisurely. You climb a little, then can stroll and chat on the terrace before continuing upwards. The stairs and terraces are wide, encouraging social interaction. The terraces allow one to adapt to the climb and to get one's bearings. From the new height and vantage point, you can look around and orient yourself to the familiar landmarks, the prior knowledge.

As everyone has guessed, you should avoid constructing the medieval staircase in the classroom. A steep, seemingly endless series of inductive steps will allow only a few to reach the conclusion at the top, and most of those few will not willingly repeat the experience. Not coincidentally, the lecture became a chief means of education in the Middle Ages (although in fairness, there were debates as well). Many classes were a steep climb through a read text. Teaching was telling.

The Socratic teacher is the Renaissance or Post-Renaissance architect, designing inductive steps that lead to personally engaged discussion on the terraces of higher level thinking. By learning how to make the steps, the students are empowered to think more analytically and creatively.

Time for Improvement

Curriculum delivery is pulled in two directions, vertically and horizontally. The horizontal pull, a kind of calendar-induced gravity, is the pressure to cover a set number of units in the 180-odd days of the school year. Within these units, one must cover an ambitious number of determined topics, concepts, skills, issues, works, experiments, problems, etc., about which the students must be assessed quantitatively. The vertical pull is the need to relate all of this material to the students on a personal level or, in reality, little authentic learning takes place. They will dash down the field and have amnesia in the end zone. Fostering authentic learning requires many teaching strategies and an acute consciousness of time. The vertical journey is not the collective boat ride from point A to point B, but the individual scuba dive between the two points.

What this means practically is that the teacher needs to envision the year clearly and choose the claims, concepts, issues, and problems that can be investigated vertically within a reasonable amount of time. One brings the class forward in the boat, but pauses regularly along the way to allow individual scuba diving to explore these claims, concepts, issues, and problems. Socratic teaching engages the individual and leads her to greater understanding, differentiating to that individual's strengths and weaknesses.

The School of Socrates

Teachers must embark on the Socratic journey together. Collaborative planning, peer coaching, reflecting on instruction, and visiting classrooms to observe and understand practice have all been identified as crucial strategies to improve instruction (Barber & Mourshed, 2007). Focusing these strategies on learning Socratic instruction ensures its growth in the school.

Today Socrates remains a very appealing figure. His method of systematic inductive questioning leads learners through personal reasoning to a meaningful discovery in higher level thinking. In many respects, his method is very modern. Practiced well, the teacher differentiates the sequence of questions to each individual learner. It is a method of authentic discovery, not shrewd debate, and leads students to more independent thinking and problem solving. A Chinese proverb says, "Teachers open the door. You enter by yourself." The Socratic Method opens the door.

REFERENCES

Adams, J. (n.d.). *Primer on teaching, with special reference to Sunday School work*. Edinburgh, Scotland: Clark.

Adler, M. J. (1946). *Manual for discussion leaders of the Great Books Program*. Chicago, IL: Chicago University Bookstore.

Adler, M. J. (1982). *The Paideia proposal: An educational manifesto*. New York, NY: Macmillan.

Adler, M. J. (1983). *Paideia problems and possibilities*. New York, NY: Macmillan.

Adler, M. J. (1984a). *The Paideia program: An educational syllabus*. New York, NY: Macmillan.

Adler, M. J. (1984b). *Six great ideas: Truth, goodness, beauty, liberty, equality, justice: Ideas we judge by, ideas we act on*. New York, NY: Collier Books.

Adler, M. J. (1992). *The great ideas: A lexicon of Western thought*. New York, NY: Macmillan.

Adler, M. J., & Van Doren, C. (1984). The conduct of seminars. In M. J. Adler (Ed.), *The Paideia program: An educational syllabus* [Kindle edition]. New York, NY: Simon & Schuster.

Anderson, L. W., Krathwohl, D. R., Airasian, P. W., Cruikshank, K. A., Mayer, R. E., Pintrich, P. R., . . . Wittrock, M. C. (Eds.) (2001). *A taxonomy for learning, teaching, and assessing: A revision of Bloom's Taxonomy of Educational Objectives*. Boston, MA: Allyn & Bacon.

Andre, C., & Velasquez, M. (1990). Justice and fairness. *Issues in Ethics, 3*(2). Retrieved from http://www.scu.edu/ethics/publications/iie/v3n2/

Areeda, P. E. (1996). The Socratic Method (SM) (Lecture at Puget Sound, 1/31/1990). *Harvard Law Review, 109*, 911–922.

Aristophanes. (2005). *The complete plays* (P. Roche, Trans.). New York, NY: New American Library. (Original work written c. 420 B.C.E.)

Baggini, J. (2002). *Making sense: Philosophy behind the headlines.* Oxford, England: Oxford University Press.

Baggini, J., & Fosl, P. S. (2010). *The philosopher's toolkit: A compendium of philosophical concepts and methods* (2nd ed.). Malden, MA: Wiley-Blackwell.

Ball, W. H., & Brewer, P. (2000). *Socratic seminars in the block.* Larchmont, NY: Eye on Education.

Barber, M., & Mourshed, M. (2007). *How the world's best performing school systems come out on top.* Retrieved from http://mckinseyonsociety.com/how-the-worlds-best-performing-schools-come-out-on-top/

Beam, A. (2008). *A great idea at the time: The rise, fall, and curious afterlife of the Great Books.* New York, NY: Public Affairs.

Benson, H. H. (2011). Socratic Method. In D. R. Morrison (Ed.), *The Cambridge companion to Socrates* (pp. 179–200). Cambridge, England: Cambridge University Press.

Betts, G. H. (1910). *The recitation.* Mount Vernon, IA: Hawk-Eye.

Bloom, B. S. (Ed.). (1956). *Taxonomy of educational objectives, handbook I: The cognitive domain.* New York, NY: David McKay.

Bond, T. (1990). *Games for social and life skills.* Cheltenham, England: Nelson Thornes.

Brandes, D. (1990a). *Gamesters' handbook: 140 games for teachers and group leaders.* Cheltenham, England: Nelson Thornes.

Brandes, D. (1990b). *Gamesters' handbook two.* Cheltenham, England: Nelson Thornes.

Brookfield, S. D., & Preskill, S. (2005). *Discussion as a way of teaching: Tools and techniques for democratic classrooms* (2nd ed.). San Francisco, CA: Jossey-Bass.

Chambers, R. (2009). *Participatory workshops: A sourcebook of 21 sets of ideas and activities.* Sterling, VA: Earthscan Publications.

Christensen, C. R., Garvin, D., & Sweet, A. (1991). *Education for judgment: The artistry of discussion leadership.* Boston, MA: Harvard Business School Press.

Copeland, M. (2005). *Socratic circles: Fostering critical and creative thinking in middle and high school.* Portland, ME: Stenhouse.

Craddock, F. B. (2001). *As one without authority.* St. Louis, MO: Chalice Press.

Diogenes Laertius. (1915). *The lives and opinions of eminent philosophers* (C. D. Yonge, Trans.). London, England: G. Bell & Sons. (Original work c. 225)

Doyle, A. C. (1905). The adventure of the dancing men. In *The return of Sherlock Holmes* (pp. 61–92). New York, NY: McClure, Phillips.

Durkin, M. C. (1993). *Thinking through class discussion: The Hilda Taba approach.* Lancaster, PA: Technomic.

Elder, L., & Paul, R. (1998). The role of Socratic questioning in thinking, teaching, and learning. *The Clearing House: A Journal of Educational Strategies, 71,* 297–301.

Fo, D. (1992). Accidental death of an anarchist. In E. Emery (Trans.), *Plays: One* (pp. 123–211). London, England: Methuen.

Freire, P. (1996). *Pedagogy of the oppressed* (M. B. Ramos, Trans.). New York, NY: Continuum.

Gardner, H. (2006). *Five minds for the future.* Boston, MA: Harvard Business School Press.

Geach, P. (1966). Plato's *Euthyphro*: An analysis and commentary. *The Monist, 50,* 369–382.

Goleman, D. (1996). *Emotional intelligence: Why it can matter more than IQ.* London, England: Bloomsbury.

Guthrie, W. K. C. (1971). *Socrates.* Cambridge, England: Cambridge University Press.

Hamilton, S. (1906). *The recitation.* Philadelphia, PA: J.B. Lippincott.

Holyoak, K. J. (2005). Analogy. In K. J. Holyoak & R. G. Morrison (Eds.), *The Cambridge handbook of thinking and reasoning* (pp. 117–142). Cambridge, England: Cambridge University Press.

Honderich, T. (Ed.). (1995). *The Oxford companion to philosophy.* Oxford, England: Oxford University Press.

Horne, H. H. (1916). *Story-telling, questioning and studying, three school arts.* New York, NY: Macmillan.

Houston, A. (Ed.). (2004). *Franklin: The autobiography and other writings on politics, economics, and virtue.* Cambridge, England: Cambridge University Press.

Jay, A. (Writer), Lynn, J. (Writer), & Lotterby, S. (Director). (1986). The grand design [Television series episode]. In Lotterby, S. (Producer), *Yes, Prime Minister.* London, England: British Broadcasting Corporation.

Johnson, J., Carlson, S., Kastl, J., & Kastl, R. (1992). Developing conceptual thinking: The concept attainment model. *The Clearing House: A Journal of Educational Strategies, 66,* 117–121.

Joyce, B., & Calhoun, E. (1998). *Learning to teach inductively.* Boston, MA: Allyn & Bacon.

Kahneman, D. (2011). *Thinking fast and slow.* New York, NY: Farrar, Straus, and Giroux.

Katz, H. E., & O'Neill, K. F. (2009). *Strategies and techniques of law school teaching: A primer for new (and not so new) professors.* New York, NY: Aspen.

Kerr, O. S. (1999). The decline of the Socratic Method at Harvard. *Nebraska Law Review, 78,* 113–134.

Kimball, B. A. (2009). *The inception of modern professional education: C. C. Langdell, 1826–1906.* Chapel Hill: University of North Carolina Press.

Krull, E. (2003, December). Hilda Taba (1902–1967). *Prospects, 33,* 481–491. Retrieved from http://www.ibe.unesco.org

Law, S. (2003). *The philosophy gym: 25 short adventures in thinking.* New York, NY: St. Martin's Press.

Law, S. (2007). *Philosophy.* London, England: Dorling Kindersley.

Lewin, K., Lippit, R., & White, R. K. (1939). Patterns of aggressive behavior in experimentally created social climates. *Journal of Social Psychology, 10,* 271–301.

Lyman, F. T. (1981). The responsive classroom discussion: The inclusion of all students. In A. Anderson (Ed.), *Mainstreaming digest* (pp. 109–113). College Park: University of Maryland Press.

Magee, B. (1998). *The story of philosophy.* London, England: Dorling Kindersley.

Mak, D. K., Mak, A. T., & Mak, A. B. (2009). *Solving everyday problems with the scientific method: Thinking like a scientist.* Hackensack, NJ: World Scientific.

McMurry, C. A., & McMurry, F. M. (1903). *The method of the recitation* (Rev. ed.). New York, NY: Macmillan.

Minchew, S. S., & Hopper, P. F. (2008). Techniques for using humor and fun in the language arts classroom. *The Clearing House: A Journal of Educational Strategies, 81,* 232–236.

Moseley, D., Baumfield, V., Elliot, J., Gregson, M., Higgins, S., Miller, J., & Newton, D. (2005). *Frameworks for thinking: A handbook for teaching and learning.* Cambridge, England: Cambridge University Press.

Myers, D. G. (2004). *Intuition, its powers and perils.* New Haven, CT: Yale University Press.

Newby, T. J., Ertmer, P. A., & Stepich, D.A. (1995). Instructional analogies and the learning of concepts. *Educational Technology Research and Development, 43*(1), 5–18.

Novak, J. D., & Gowin, D. B. (1984). *Learning how to learn.* New York, NY: Cambridge University Press.

Nussbaum, M. C. (2010). *Not for profit: Why the democracy needs the humanities.* Princeton, NJ: Princeton University Press.

Parker, S. C. (1920). *Methods of teaching in high schools.* Boston, MA: Ginn and Company.

Paul, R., & Elder, L. (2007a). Critical thinking: The art of Socratic questioning. *Journal of Developmental Education, 31*(1), 36–37.

Paul, R., & Elder, L. (2007b). Critical thinking: The art of Socratic questioning, part II. *Journal of Developmental Education, 31*(2), 32–33.

Paul, R., & Elder, L. (2008). Critical thinking: The art of Socratic questioning, part III. *Journal of Developmental Education, 31*(3), 34–35.

Phillips, J. D. (1948). Report on discussion 66. *Adult Education Journal, 7,* 181–182.

Plato. (1997a). Alcibiades (D. S. Hutchinson, Trans.). In J. M. Cooper (Ed.), *Complete works* (pp. 557–595). Indianapolis, IN: Hackett.

Plato. (1997b). Apology (G. M. A. Grube, Trans.). In J. M. Cooper (Ed.), *Complete works* (pp. 17–36). Indianapolis, IN: Hackett.

Plato. (1997c). Charmides. In J. M. Cooper (Ed.), *Complete works* (pp. 639–663). Indianapolis, IN: Hackett.

Plato. (1997d). Euthydemus (R. K. Sprague, Trans.). In J. M. Cooper (Ed.), *Complete works* (pp. 708–745). Indianapolis, IN: Hackett.

Plato. (1997e). Euthyphro (G. M. A. Grube, Trans.). In J. M. Cooper (Ed.), *Complete works* (pp. 1–16). Indianapolis, IN: Hackett.

Plato. (1997f). Gorgias (D. J. Zeyl, Trans.). In J. M. Cooper (Ed.), *Complete works* (pp. 791–869). Indianapolis, IN: Hackett.

Plato. (1997g). Laches. (R. K. Sprague, Trans.). In J. M. Cooper (Ed.), *Complete works* (pp. 664–687). Indianapolis, IN: Hackett.

Plato. (1997h). Lysis (S. Lombardo, Trans.). In J. M. Cooper (Ed.), *Complete works* (pp. 687–707). Indianapolis, IN: Hackett.

Plato. (1997i). Meno (G. M. A. Grube, Trans.). In J. M. Cooper (Ed.), *Complete works* (pp. 870–897). Indianapolis, IN: Hackett.

Plato. (1997j). Phaedo (G. M. A. Grube, Trans.). In J. M. Cooper (Ed.), *Complete works* (pp. 49–100). Indianapolis, IN: Hackett.

Plato. (1997k). Protagoras (S. Lombardo & K. Bell, Trans.). In J. M. Cooper (Ed.), *Complete works* (pp. 746–790). Indianapolis, IN: Hackett.

Plato. (1997l). Symposium (A. Nehamas & P. Woodruff, Trans.). In J. M. Cooper (Ed.), *Complete works* (pp. 457–505). Indianapolis, IN: Hackett.

Plato. (1997m). Theaetetus (M. J. Levett, Trans.). In J. M. Cooper (Ed.), *Complete works* (pp. 157–234). Indianapolis, IN: Hackett.

Pólya, G., & Anning, N. (1935). How to look for the solution. *National Mathematics Magazine, 9,* 172–173.

Pólya, G. (1957). *How to solve it: A new aspect of mathematical method* (Rev. ed.). Princeton: Princeton University Press. (Original work published 1945)

Pólya, G., & Szegö, G. (1998). *Problems and theorems in analysis I* (D. Aeppli, Trans.). New York, NY: Springer. (Original work published 1972)

Postman, N., & Weingartner, C. (1969). *Teaching as a subversive activity.* New York, NY: Delacorte Press.

Powell, B. (1995). Memorial: A defense of the Socratic Method: An interview with Martin B. Louis (1934–94). *North Carolina Law Review, 73,* 957–987.

Ragsdale, S., & Saylor, A. (2007). *Great group games: 175 boredom-busting, zero-prep team builders for all ages.* Minneapolis, MN: Search Institute Press.

Robinson, R. (1953). *Plato's earlier dialectic.* New York, NY: Garland Publishing.

Ryle, G. (1966). *Plato's progress.* Cambridge, England: Cambridge University Press.

Seeskin, K. (1987). *Dialogue and discovery. A study in Socratic Method.* Albany: State University of New York Press.

Stanford, G. (1977). *Developing effective classroom groups: A practical guide for teachers.* New York, NY: Hart.

Stanford, G., & Stanford, B. D. (1969). *Learning discussion skills through games.* New York, NY: Citation Press.

Sternberg, R. J., & Grigorenko, E. L. (2004). Successful intelligence in the classroom. *Theory Into Practice, 43,* 274–280.

Sternberg, R. J. (2013). Reform education: Teach wisdom and ethics. *Phi Delta Kappan 94*(7), 44–47.

Stock, G. (2004). *The kids' book of questions.* New York, NY: Workman.

Taba, H. (1967). *Teacher's handbook for elementary social studies.* Palo Alto, CA: Addison-Wesley.

Terkel, S. (n.d.). *Saul Alinksy, the father of community organizing, in this own words . . .* Retrieved from http://www.marinkapeschmann.com/2012/04/21/saul-alinsky-the-father-of-community-organizing-in-this-own-words-audio/

Thoreau, H. D. (1992). On civil disobedience. In B. Atkinson (Ed.), *Walden and other writings of Henry David Thoreau* (pp. 665–693). New York, NY: The Modern Library. (Original work published 1849)

Torok, S. E, McMorris, R. F., & Lin, W. (2004). Is humor an appreciated teaching tool? Perceptions of professors' teaching styles and use of humor. *College Teaching, 52*(1), 14–20.

Turkle, S. (2012). *Connected, but alone?* [Video]. Retrieved from http://www.ted.com/talks/sherry_turkle_alone_together.html

Twain, M. (1917). *What is man? and other essays.* New York, NY: Harper and Brothers.

Vlastos, G. (1994). The Socratic elenchus: Method is all. In M. Burnyeat (Ed.), *Socratic studies* (pp. 1–37). Cambridge, England: Cambridge University Press.

Wagner, T. (2008). *The global achievement gap: Why even our best schools don't teach the new survival skills our children need—and what we can do about it.* New York, NY: Basic Books.

Warburton, N. (2004). *Philosophy: The basics.* London, England: Routledge.

Warren, E. H. (1942). *A spartan education.* Boston, MA: Houghton Mifflin.

Watts, I. (1741). *The improvement of the mind: Or, a supplement to the art of logick: Containing a variety of remarks and rules for the attainment and communication of useful knowledge, in religion, in the sciences, and in common life.* London, England: Printed for James Brackstone at the Globe in Cornhill.

West, E. (1999). *The big book of icebreakers: 50 quick, fun activities for energizing meetings and workshops.* New York, NY: McGraw-Hill.

Wiggins, G., & McTighe, J. (2011). *The understanding by design guide to creating high-quality units.* Alexandria, VA: Association for Supervision and Curriculum Development.

Wormeli, R. (2009). *Metaphors & analogies: Power tools for teaching any subject.* Portland, ME: Stenhouse.

Wright, L. B. (1943, July). Thomas Jefferson and the classics. *Proceedings of the American Philosophical Society, 87,* 223–233.

Xenophon. (1994). *Memorabilia* (A. L. Bonnette, Trans.). Ithaca, NY: Cornell University Press. (Original work published c. 371 B.C.E.)

Zahler, K. A. (2010). *McGraw-Hill's MAT: Miller Analogies Test* (2nd ed.). New York, NY: McGraw-Hill.

FURTHER READING

There is a great deal to read about Socrates and the Socratic Method, although the literature on the latter generally is not directed to pedagogy or the classroom teacher. Among many other works, I have consulted Benson (2011), Vlastos (1994), Seeskin (1987), Guthrie (1969), Ryle (1966), and Robinson (1953, 1980). I believe the work by Guthrie remains the most lucid and complete critical summary of many basic issues (although later scholars will disagree with some findings), and the volume by Ryle the most enjoyable treatment (if offering conjectures that have not found wide consensus).

The major split in the scholarly literature, noted by Seeskin, is whether to treat the Platonic dialogues purely as philosophy or as literature (Seeskin, 1987). In general, while all the scholarly literature provides insights in myriad directions, one can learn more regarding pedagogy from reading the original ancient works by Plato and Xenophon, keeping in mind that the dialogues are not transcriptions, the use of inductive questioning varies, and Socrates was not the perfect teacher (if such exists).

Regarding the texts of Plato, I have used the edition by Cooper (1997a–1997m). In my text I have followed the practice of citing the Stephanus numbers.

Regarding the texts of Xenophon, I have used both the 1994 translation as well as the earlier translation by Dalkyn.

PLANNING
TEMPLATES

Socratic Dialogue Planning Sheet 1: Objectives and Elements

Class: _____

Date: _____

Concept/Issue/Problem: _____

Objective: _____

ELEMENTS NEEDED
Inductive Questions

_____

_____

_____

Analogies

_____

_____

_____

Examples

_____

_____

_____

Counterexamples

_____

_____

_____

Hypotheticals

_____

_____

_____

Socratic Dialogue Planning Sheet 2: Definitions and Key Terms

Class: _____

Date: _____

Concept/Issue/Problem: _____

Objective: _____

DEFINITIONS: Write out the definitions and key terms in words the students will understand. Record the source of the definition.

_____

_____

_____

_____

_____

_____

_____

_____

_____

_____

_____

_____

_____

_____

_____

_____

_____

_____

_____

_____

Socratic Dialogue Planning Sheet 3:
Research and Key Points

Class: _____

Date: _____

Concept/Issue/Problem: _____

Objective: _____

RESEARCH: Record here any research made, noting as well the source used. Other sheets may be needed. After reflection, write down the key points for the dialogue.

Further reflect on the information from the Student Preparation Sheet regarding the difficulties students have encountered. How will you address their difficulties?

_____

_____

_____

_____

_____

_____

_____

_____

_____

_____

_____

_____

_____

_____

_____

_____

_____

_____

Socratic Dialogue Planning Sheet 4: Brainstorming

Class: _____

Date: _____

Concept/Issue/Problem: _____

Objective: _____

BRAINSTORMING: Keeping in mind the objectives, concept and/or key ideas, and research, brainstorm further elements for the dialogue (questions, analogies, examples, counter-examples, hypotheticals). Use concept mapping, lists, flow charts, or another method.

_____

_____

_____

_____

_____

_____

_____

_____

_____

_____

_____

_____

_____

_____

_____

_____

_____

_____

_____

_____

_____

Socratic Dialogue Planning Sheet 5:
Inductive Outline

Class: _____

Date: _____

Concept/Issue/Problem: _____

Objective: _____

INDUCTIVE OUTLINE: Using the key points, definitions as well as other information and elements from research, brainstorming, and reflection to draft the inductive outline. Other sheets may be needed.

_____

_____

_____

_____

_____

_____

_____

_____

_____

_____

_____

_____

_____

_____

_____

_____

_____

_____

_____

Socratic Dialogue Planning Sheet 6:
Teaching Reflection

Class: _____

Date: _____

Concept/Issue/Problem: _____

Objective: _____

TEACHING REFLECTION: Reflect on whether and how the objectives of the dialogue were met. How did students respond? What went well? What needed improvement?

_____

_____

_____

_____

_____

_____

_____

_____

_____

_____

_____

_____

_____

_____

_____

_____

_____

_____

_____

_____

Student Preparation Sheet for Socratic Dialogue

Name: _____

Class: _____

Date: _____

Concept/Issue/Problem: _____

Objective: _____

Please reflect and make notes on the following questions in preparation for class dialogue.

1. Define the concept or the key terms of the issue or problem in your own words. Give examples or make analogies to clarify your thoughts.

    _____

    _____

    _____

    _____

    _____

    _____

    _____

    _____

2. What did you find difficult or confusing in thinking about this concept, issue, or problem? Please write this on a separate piece of paper and return to me by _____.

    _____

    _____

    _____

    _____

    _____

    _____

    _____

Socratic Discussion Planning Sheet

Class: _____

Date: _____

Concept/Issue/Problem: _____

Objective: _____

OPENING

_____

_____

_____

EXPLORATORY QUESTIONS

_____

_____

_____

_____

_____

_____

CONCLUDING QUESTION

_____

_____

_____

EXTENDED ACTIVITY
- Analytical

_____

_____

- Practical

_____

_____

- Creative

_____

_____

Student Preparation Sheet for Socratic Discussion

Name: _____

Class: _____

Date: _____

Concept/Issue/Problem: _____

Objective: _____

Please reflect and make notes on the following questions in preparation for class discussion.

Question 1:

_____

_____

_____

_____

_____

_____

_____

_____

Question 2:

_____

_____

_____

_____

_____

_____

_____

_____

Question 3: What did you find difficult or confusing in this text? Please write this on a separate piece of paper and return to me by _____.

SUGGESTIONS FOR DISCUSSION TEXTS

Texts may be predefined by the curriculum, but there are many resources for further investigation. For instance, the Academy of American Poets has a website suggesting poems for teaching (http://www.poets.org). Short films or animations (anything from 1 to 30 minutes) have rapidly matured, and there are several excellent international competitions hosted on the internet (e.g., http://www.filminute.com). TED.Ed has wonderfully brief and engaging lessons (http://ed.ted.com). Khan Academy also offers a broad range of materials (http://www.khanacademy.org).

I will recommend only one book, Stephen Law's, *The Philosophy Gym: 25 Short Adventures in Thinking* (2003). Illustrated by Daniel Postgate, it presents small dialogues and explanations on a wide variety of concepts, issues, and problems. It is a smart and accessible book that challenges students to think better about important things.

Below I have listed articles, art works, documentaries, and speeches or presentations that may be discussed in the classroom. Many more from a wide variety of cultures and times could be included. As always, preview and prepare everything before presenting it in the classroom.

Articles

- ഏ Somini Sengupta, "Free speech in the age of Youtube," *The New York Times* (22 September 2012).

- ഏ Ann Landers, "Animal experiments benefit humanity," *The Chicago Tribune* (6 October 1988).

- Jeffrey Goldberg, "Why liberals should support armed self-defense," *Bloomberg.com* (5 March 2013).

- Mike Norman, "If the lottery is in trouble, so is Texas," *Star-Telegram* (25 April 2013).

- "Too much homework," *The Suburban.com* (2009).

- "Grounding the drones: Iowa City gets a vote on banning airborne spies," *The Washington Times* (8 April 2013).

- Alan Dershowitz, "Warming up to torture?" *The Los Angeles Times* (17 October 2006).

- Carl Bernstein, "The idiot culture," *The New Republic* (8 June 1992). http://www.carlbernstein.com.

- Charles Krauthammer, "Pushing the envelope, NSA-style," *The Washington Post* (14 June 2013).

Art

- Guerrilla Girls, *The Advantages of Being a Woman Artist* (poster), 1988.

- *Meditating Buddha*, from Gandhara, Pakistan. 2nd century C.E.

- *Shiva as Nataraja*, c.1000.

- Great Mosque, Damascus, Syria, 706–715.

- Great Mosque, Córdoba, Spain, 961–965.

- Pablo Picasso, *Guernica*, 1937.

- Gislebertus, *Last Judgment*, c.1120–1135.

- Salvador Dalí, *The Persistence of Memory*, 1931.

- Ben Shahn, *The Passion of Sacco and Vanzetti*, 1931.

- Francisco Goya, *Saturn Devouring One of His Children*, 1819–1823.

- Théodore Géricault, *Raft of the Medusa*, 1818–1819.

- Venus of Willendorf, 28,000 BCE

- Cave paintings, Chauvet, 28,000 BCE

- Raphael, *The School of Athens*, c.1510–1512

- Michelangelo, *The Sistine Chapel Ceiling*, 1508–1512

- Leonardo da Vinci, *Mona Lisa*, c.1503–1506.

- Caravaggio, *The Calling of Saint Matthew*, 1599–1600.
- Rembrandt, *Self-Portrait*, 1669.
- Eugène Delacroix, *Liberty Leading the People*, 1830.
- Vincent Van Gogh, *Starry Night*, 1889.
- Jacob Lawrence, *Tombstones*, 1942.
- José Clemente Orozco, *American Civilization—The Gods of the Modern World*, 1932.
- Bill Viola, *The Crossing*, 1996.
- Maya Ying Lin, *Vietnam War Memorial*, 1981–1983.
- Lucian Freud, *HM Queen Elizabeth II*, 2000–2001.

Documentaries

- Heidi Ewing and Rachel Grady (Directors), *Jesus Camp*, 2006.
- Robert Kenner (Director), *Food, Inc.*, 2008.
- Werner Herzog (Director), *Cave of Forgotten Dreams*, 2010.
- Davis Guggenheim (Director), *An Inconvenient Truth*, 2006.
- Vicki Abeles and Jessica Congdon (Directors), *Race to Nowhere*, 2009.
- Steve James (Director), *Hoop Dreams*, 1994.
- Carl Hindmarch (Director), *Simon Schama's Power of Art: Caravaggio*, 2006.
- Frederick Wiseman (Director), *High School*, 1968.
- Jacques Perrin and Jacques Cluzaud (Directors), *Oceans*, 2009.
- Anthony Waller, Toshi Hoo, and Raymond Kurzweil (Directors). *The Singularity Is Near*, 2010.
- Bess Kargman (Director), *First Position*, 2011.
- Kate Dart (Director), *The Creative Brain: How Insight Works*, 2013.

Speeches / Presentations

- Abraham Lincoln, The Gettysburg Address, 1863.
- Martin Luther King, Jr., "I Have a Dream," 1963.

- ஃ Martin Luther King, Jr., "I've Been to the Mountaintop," 1968.
- ஃ Maya Angelou, Eulogy for Coretta Scott King, 2006.
- ஃ Aung San Suu Kyi, "Freedom From Fear," 1990.
- ஃ Lyndon Baines Johnson, "We Shall Overcome," 1965.
- ஃ Franklin Delano Roosevelt, First Inaugural Address, 1933.
- ஃ Franklin Delano Roosevelt, Second Bill of Rights, 1944.
- ஃ Toni Morrison, Nobel Speech, 1993.
- ஃ Jane Goodall, "What Separates Us From the Apes," 2002.
- ஃ Ursula LeGuin, Bryn Mawr Commencement Address, 1986.
- ஃ Steve Jobs, Stanford Commencement Address, 2005.
- ஃ Hans Rosling, "Stats That Reshape Your Worldview," 2006.
- ஃ Doris Lessing, "On Not Winning the Nobel Prize," 2007.
- ஃ Sir Ken Robinson, "Changing Education Paradigms," 2010.
- ஃ Paul Root Wolpe, "It's Time to Question Bio-Engineering," 2010.
- ஃ Michael Specter, "The Danger of Science Denial," 2010.
- ஃ Salman Khan, "Let's Use Video to Reinvent Education," 2011.
- ஃ Amy Cuddy, "Your Body Language Shapes Who You Are," 2012.
- ஃ Sherry Turkle, "Connected But Alone?" 2012.

ABOUT THE AUTHOR

Erick Wilberding, Ph.D., is a teacher at an international school in Rome, Italy, with nearly 20 years of teaching experience in middle school and high school. He received his doctorate in art history from the Institute of Fine Arts of New York University.

COMMON CORE STATE STANDARDS ALIGNMENT

Menu	Common Core State Standards
Chapter 5: Cultivating Gadflies	
Lesson 1, p. 80	English Language Arts Standards: Reading: Informational Text. Standard 2: Determine a central idea of a text and analyze its development over the course of the text, including its relationship to supporting ideas; provide an objective summary of the text.
	English Language Arts Standards: Reading: Informational Text. Standard 8: Delineate and evaluate the argument and specific claims in a text, assessing whether the reasoning is sound and the evidence is relevant and sufficient; recognize when irrelevant evidence is introduced.
	English Language Arts Standards: Speaking & Listening. Comprehension and Collaboration: Standard 1a: Come to discussions prepared, having read or researched material under study; explicitly draw on that preparation by referring to evidence on the topic, text, or issue to probe and reflect on ideas under discussion.
	English Language Arts Standards: Speaking & Listening. Comprehension and Collaboration: Standard 3: Delineate a speaker's argument and specific claims, evaluating the soundness of the reasoning and relevance and sufficiency of the evidence and identifying when irrelevant evidence is introduced.

Menu	Common Core State Standards
Lesson 2, p. 82	English Language Arts Standards: Reading: Informational Text. Standard 2: Determine a central idea of a text and analyze its development over the course of the text, including its relationship to supporting ideas; provide an objective summary of the text.
	English Language Arts Standards: Reading: Informational Text. Standard 8: Delineate and evaluate the argument and specific claims in a text, assessing whether the reasoning is sound and the evidence is relevant and sufficient; recognize when irrelevant evidence is introduced.
	English Language Arts Standards: Speaking & Listening. Comprehension and Collaboration: Standard 1a: Come to discussions prepared, having read or researched material under study; explicitly draw on that preparation by referring to evidence on the topic, text, or issue to probe and reflect on ideas under discussion.
	English Language Arts Standards: Speaking & Listening. Comprehension and Collaboration: Standard 3: Delineate a speaker's argument and specific claims, evaluating the soundness of the reasoning and relevance and sufficiency of the evidence and identifying when irrelevant evidence is introduced.
Lesson 3, p. 85	English Language Arts Standards: Reading: Informational Text. Standard 2: Determine a central idea of a text and analyze its development over the course of the text, including its relationship to supporting ideas; provide an objective summary of the text.
	English Language Arts Standards: Reading: Informational Text. Standard 5: Analyze in detail the structure of a specific paragraph in a text, including the role of particular sentences in developing and refining a key concept.
	English Language Arts Standards: Reading: Informational Text. Standard 8: Delineate and evaluate the argument and specific claims in a text, assessing whether the reasoning is sound and the evidence is relevant and sufficient; recognize when irrelevant evidence is introduced.
	English Language Arts Standards: Speaking & Listening. Comprehension and Collaboration: Standard 1a: Come to discussions prepared, having read or researched material under study; explicitly draw on that preparation by referring to evidence on the topic, text, or issue to probe and reflect on ideas under discussion.

Menu	Common Core State Standards
Lesson 3, p. 85, *continued*	English Language Arts Standards: Speaking & Listening. Comprehension and Collaboration: Standard 3: Delineate a speaker's argument and specific claims, evaluating the soundness of the reasoning and relevance and sufficiency of the evidence and identifying when irrelevant evidence is introduced.